Loving U Was My Addiction...
But Missing U...

Loving U Was My Addiction...
But Missing U...

Sandip Gyanaprakash

GenNext Publication

First Published, 2018

Published by

GenNext Publication
5, Ansari Road
Daryaganj, New Delhi-110002
Phone: 9811692060
E-mail: gennextpublication@hotmail.com

Printed at: G. Print Process, Delhi.

Cataloging in Publication Data—DK

Courtesy: D.K. Agencies (P) Ltd. <docinfo@dkagencies.com>

Gyanaprakash, Sandip, author.

Loving u was my addiction....... but missing u..... / by Sandip Gyanaprakash.

pages cm

Novel.

ISBN: 978-93-5324-129-2

1. Romance fiction, Indic (English) I. Title.

LCC PR9499.4.G93L68 2018 | DDC 823.92 23

Acknowledgement

Were it not these people I thank below, this book would still be resting in my wardrobe with a layer of dust on it. Of course thanking God for his blessings to get my work published.

Firstly I would thank my Grand Mother for all her love and care she showed when I was writing this book. I would thank my parents to trust me that I could actually do something in my life. I would thank my grandfather, ShyamSundar Jena to teach me how to frame a sentence in English Language, my first grammar teacher.

I would thank my tutor Mr. ChittaRanjan Das for his dedication and his continuous reminders to get my work published. Dr. S.N Tripathy, my first editor who made me believe that I can get published. My only two school friends Siddharth and Deepanwita who dared to go through my manuscript.

Mayank obviously, Bro I miss you. Rohan Singh, Monalisha Paul and Simran who are still in a state of shock hearing that I can write. Worse, get published!! Of course Neelam and Aditi my sweethearts who pushed me everyday to the publishers offices all round Delhi. Raghav for his attitude " Bhaitu hi he apnalekhak". My gang, thanks a lot for your support, without you this was not possible.

My family and friends, who have supported me constantly. If at all I have missed someone. Thanks a lot for all your support.

Prologue

"Bye dude. Take care", said Raghav

"Oh sure, but you take care of my sweet hearts!!" I told Rohan, pointing at Sweety, Aditi and Neel

"Take care, son. And do not disturb Uncle in his work", Mom said as we were in the Railway station. I was leaving for New Delhi. I had decided to learn some corporate tricks from my mom's younger brother. He was a flourishing entrepreneur of a company in the capital of the country. He had employed over fifty employees.

I said goodbye to Rohan, Raghav, Sweety, Aditi, Neel, Mom and Dad boarding the Samparkranti express. As soon as I entered my bogie, my eyes saw something hotter than chilli flakes. I found a huge bevy of young and hot Punjabi girls accommodating the whole bogie, leaving apart just a few outsiders who did not belong to their group. I was one of those advantageous outsiders. On enquiring I found that they had been to Odisha for the national sports event, representing their university. I had nothing to do with that, I knew I will not be bored at least till I reach the New Delhi station. As soon as the train moved I waved my hand bidding good bye to my friends and parents. I could see Rohan winking at me and I knew the reason he did that. I am sure he heartily envied my travel with the bunch of hotties.

I soon had friendship with the girls in my compartment. We started flirting with each other, not because I was a handsome guy but because I was the only young guy in the whole bogie. The rest were either families with uncles and aunties or old people all around the bogie, with the pretty girls. I chatted with almost all of them. They told me all about their visit to Odisha, the prizes they won, the places they visited and many others. They wanted to know more about the place and I was ready to boast about my own state. I shared some funny incidents and stuffs about my university (Ravenshaw University). They even shared facts about their university and state. I didn't have time to get bored the whole day. We had shared our food and thoughts. Few of them had boy friends; few others did not have one.

Finally came the worst part of the travel. Time to sleep!! I didn't want to sleep, so I took the corner seat, switched on my seat lamp and started reading my favourite horror novel.

Suddenly the prettiest girl of the group came towards me. She had not spoken a single word to me during the whole day. I had kept asking myself the same question again and again. Why didn't she want to talk to me? I didn't have any answer for that. But maybe it was my good luck, I never knew. She had eagle like eyes, fair skin and very attractive lips with a heavy amount of lip gloss on them. With a height of around five feet four inches, she looked like a model. She had the-perfect-figure which could easily hypnotize every boy's eye. Her cleavage was visible in her sexy looking night suit, which added spice to the spicy Punjabi curry. Over all she looked unquestionably stunning.

"Can I share the seat with you? I hope you are not going to sleep, you know I do not want to sleep but in the sleeper we have to because others…" she spoke but I interrupted

"Just relax. You can share my seat. Even I do not have the habit of sleeping early", I said as she sat next to me facing the window.

"Hi I am Gyan", I introduced myself

"Hello, I am Lucy Singh", she did the same in return

"Lucy Singh!! That sounds nice. Why didn't you talk to me when others were interacting with me?" I asked and I knew it sounded stupid. But I needed to start a conversation.

"That's because you were busy with them", she said and smiled. And it was a million dollar smile, as I had not seen her smile before. She was busy in her own world the whole day.

"Did you win any medal in the contest?" I asked

"Yes, I won gold medal in shooting hundred meters and a silver in fifty meters", she said with pride in her voice.

"So, you are a shooter!!!!" I exclaimed

"My dad was in the army so I have some shooting practice", she justified

"Okay, do you have a boy friend?" I asked

"No, many proposed to me but I never had any interest in making one." She said, and then taking a pause, she asked "Do you have a girl friend?"

"No, I am single" I said

"Any past?" she fired the volcanic question at me. I had expected this one, but not so early.

"Yes, I have a past. But my past is really pathetic", I declared

"Hey, I would love to listen to your past" she said with full of excitement filled in her voice, taking full control of me.

"I told you, it's really pathetic" I tried to protect myself from going to my past.

"I won't mind, please!!" she requested sweetly extending her last word to such an extent as kids do for a chocolate. To some extent it reminded me of my past.

"Okay, but promise me you will not ask any further questions after I narrate you my story" I demanded

"Done. It's a deal" she said with all her excitement sprouting out. I was forced to tell her about my love life. I looked at my wrist watch and it showed 12.00 midnight.

****

Chapter - 1

We are all living in a very complicated world. Before starting my book, these are few examples to prove that we are really living in a complicated world. If swimming is a good exercise to stay fit, then why are whales fat? Why that is everyone wants to go to heaven, but no one wants to die? Shall I say that there is a racial discrimination in chess, as the white piece is moved first? In our country we have freedom for speech then why telephone bills? If money doesn't grow in trees then why do banks have branches? Why a round pizza does come in a square box? Why doesn't glue stick to its own bottle? Why do we still call it a building when it is already built? If it's true that we are here to help others then why are others here for? If you are not supposed to drink and drive then why do bars have a parking space? Seriously!!! We are funny people living in a critically funny world.

I am an average looking guy but always had a feeling of an uncomplicated man. It was the year; I still remember when I was moving from the perilous age of teenage towards my adulthood. I did not know much about the world. But I was not just a chap who would be easily shoved away by any man. I had a killer brain which could easily trap a girl. But is it that any time I will really fall into the ditch of true love. Is there anything called true love in this world? And if something like that is there then does it exist in the present civilization? If it exists in the civilization, can it happen in college life? There are many such questions to be answered. And may be my readers are the best judges to answer these questions.

"Hey Killer lets go somewhere outside" Sweety said looking at me as we were sitting with all our group members in the classroom. Our group included four boys named Mayank, Rohan, Raghav and Gyan (me) and three girls Neel, Sweety and Aditi. We were the only students in the classroom, as our final exam for the year was approaching. We were the most sincere students of the class. We were present there even when no one else attended, or in other words when the professor was not there in the classroom for a lecture.

"Yes sure why not? Let's go to the temple outside the college gate" I spoke stupidly without exactly understanding Sweety's intensions.

"Shut up Gyan. I meant we need a break. So let's travel somewhere outside the state" Sweety suggested

"She is drunk early in the morning" Rohan commented making fun of Sweety's statement.

"Donkey!!! Listen to me first..." Sweety was trying to speak when Mayank interrupted her.

"Yes you can speak dear, we are ready to listen" Mayank tried to pull her leg and we started laughing. Pulling legs are one of the foremost jobs in college. Life is almost crumbled to rubble without it.

"I don't have to tell you anything" she said with anger flowing out of her mouth, like hot lava during a volcanic eruption. She tried to move out of the classroom. But Mayank managed to pull her back into the classroom.

"Now everyone is going to listen to what she is trying to speak. And no interference while she is speaking" Raghav announced as the grand fathers usually throw orders on their grand children. Every one nodded in agreement with a deceiving smile on their face. It seemed like a fantasy story was going to be narrated.

"Listen Guys we are going to complete our junior college and get into some other, for our higher education. So let's take a break before we are separated" She said

"She has a point" Neel said supporting her statement.

"But will it be possible for all of us to go" Rohan asked for a confirmation with a low voice. He knew it well that it was a tough job convincing his mom.

"I don't know if my mom is going to allow me" I said as I was sailing in the same boat as Rohan. My mom always proved to be an elder sister to Hitler when such matters came up.

"Okay." Sweety said taking a deliberate pause "Then, let's make a condition" she continued

"What more condition do you have?" Rohan asked with a stressful voice

"The condition is that" she said taking a deliberate pause again to increase everyone's anxiety. Uuff!! God I hated her habit of creating this suspense. "If one of us is not going then none of us will be going" she added and all of us started starring at each other's face. Now this expected fantasy tale was getting serious.

"Agreed??" she asked for confirmation. I was dreadfully confused but I gave the agreement as all others had already agreed to her condition.

"Okay, but you have to convince my mom" I said looking at Sweety

"Don't worry about that, Aditi is going to do the job. She does well convincing people" she said and relaxed me. I didn't want all of them to suffer because of me. Rohan and I were the only person in the group who had a chance of getting a negative response from the families.

"Done. Tonight, we are going to celebrate this idea in the discotheque" Raghav proposed

"Done. That's it. We are going to have a rocking party tonight" Mayank said

"But exams..." I tried to speak but no one was in a mood to listen to me.

"What exams? We have been taking exams throughout our life." Neel said

"Shut up, this is going to be the last party before exams. Done?" Rohan said extending his last word asking for a confirmation from me. His eyes were concentrating on mine without a blink. I didn't have any other option other than nodding a yes like a puppet. Even if I would have refused they would have planned the party and dragged me for it.

That evening we had a big party. Every one of us was heavily drunk in the disco. Although I don't know what exactly the case was but I remember Mayank was slapped by a girl because he was misbehaving with her in drunken state. He even didn't remember the next day what he had exactly done to the girl. The whole night we sat in our car outside the disco. No one was in a condition to drive. So I had suggested staying there till one of us was completely back to the senses and fit enough to drive us safely back to our places. Everyone had agreed to my suggestion.

Exam time came closer and every student could be seen with a tensed face. Silence, is the best answer for all questions and smile, the best reaction for all situations but unfortunately none of these works during any written exams or viva. Everyone seemed to be carrying heavy weight rice bags on their heads. All tensed faces around the campus but our group was the only one with the jolliest mood. I was the most studious student of our group. With a lot of effort I could come close to the average students mark but the rest were below average. They were still happier than me. I didn't know why?

The day of exam finally came. All the faces were distraught including mine. I had used the washroom at least ten times since the morning. Our exam centre was a different college. It was the first day of our exam. As soon as we reached all our group members got accumulated in a place. Raghav and Mayank seemed as if they were heavily drunk the previous night. But they were actually not. They had been burning the midnight oil, the whole night, for the first time in college life. So the intensive study had made their eyes seem like drunken fools.

"Where is the washroom?" I asked

"How many times do you need a washroom idiot?" Neel shouted

"Please shut up. You will not understand my condition" I justified very gently without showing any anger even though I wanted to exhibit some. But at the same time I wanted to stay cool at least till my papers were over.

"There is a bush" Rohan said pointing at a bush which was hundred meters away from us. I was slackened when I saw that. I ran behind the bush. Nothing can be more satisfying than getting a bush when you really need it. Why do people cut bushes? They are so beneficial to a man.

It took a month's time for our exams to get over. The hectic days were over and the days for enjoyment had come, till the results were out. The time had come that we seriously thought about Sweety's plan of moving somewhere outside Odisha (our native state). As per her promise Aditi was successful in convincing my mom. One evening after a long session of interaction with me, my mom finally nodded her head in allowance of my visit. Although she didn't want me to travel alone with my friends but some of my emotional dialogues forced her to agree with me. I am always good to carry people out of the world with my emotions. We booked tickets and rooms in hotels through the internet. It was very exciting. The place decided was Jammu and Kashmir, the land of apples.

It was difficult convincing Rohan's mom. She was a single parent after she had divorced her husband. She had divorced her husband because of his extra marital affairs. Rohan started hating his dad and learned living his life without him. She had to take care of Rohan with all her efforts. Rohan was the only support she had. None in her family supported her. Rohan sometimes missed his dad. So he used to call him from different numbers changing his SIM cards just to hear his voice. But he never spoke a single word when his dad picked up the call.

Rohan's mom thought Kashmir was a risky place to send her offspring. Aditi took a longer time to convince her but her power of convincing didn't fail. She was successful in booking Rohan's ticket to Kashmir. Only both of us had a problem with the family acceptance to the visit, the rests were away from it i.e we were the only two black sheep in the group who were finally successful with Aditi's support.

* * * *

Chapter - 2

I was just out of my junior college and I had a chance of moving out of the state (Odisha) with my friends to Jammu and Kashmir. I just hoped I would get someone to flirt with or it would be a damn boring visit. I had always heard of people having girlfriends and boyfriends but I believed flirting was the best medicine to any disease of a youngster. I had even visualized lovers personally in parks, shopping malls and many other public places. The best way of seeing couples was the television screen. What would have been a better place to see the love birds other than the idiot box? They looked very stupid to me. And I didn't want to look as stupid as them.

The day came when we were waiting at the railway station for our train to Jammu. We bid goodbye to our parents. We enjoyed a lot while entering the train. We had to make a long travel of a day and half. But it isn't difficult when friends are with you. It was a great feeling of going out with your friends alone without any parental restrictions.

"Hey I have something for you guys" Mayank said as the train started moving away from the platform and started opening his bag. I could see two large bottles of Rum, two bottle of same size containing whisky, another two bottles containing vodka and a Jonny walker Black Label, my favourite. I knew it was just for me.

"WOW!!!! That looks amazing dude" Neel said with such excitement as if her mouth would start watering at close quarters.

"But is it going to be sufficient for the train journey" Mayank said with dissatisfaction. He didn't think it was going to be enough for us. As a matter of fact we were heavy drunkards.

"Yes sure don't worry. We can't be out of control at least when we are travelling, so it's going to do" I egged on him.

"I also have to show you something" Rohan said with an excitement pouring out of his voice.

"What?" all of us asked in unison and he opened his bag. What my eyes could see was almost fifteen to twenty packets of our favourite flavoured cigarettes. My eyes could never get the exact count of the things until I sat down to count it.

These small things always made us happy. Friends, alcohol and cigarettes had become our life since all of us were together.

"But how can you smoke in the train? We may be fined for this" Raghav said grimly.

"Don't worry we can smoke in the rest room without anyone's knowledge. I have already done this before" Rohan justified as a well experienced train smoker.

The day went on smoothly. It was a very relaxing day. There were two girls near our berth. We had a good time flirting with them. They also seemed enjoying flirting with us. Neel and Aditi started flirting with the male members who were near us. We knew it could have caused a problem later but it is always adventurous when you are not with your parents. The day came to an end and we had completed half the packets brought by Rohan in the toilet. We had smoked a lot and I could smell the smoke of the cigarette in our bogie.

We had our home made dinner sent by my mom, Rohan's mom and some stuff prepared by Sweety. The clock had struck 10.00 pm and everyone in the train had captured their berths for a sound sleep. It was time for us to have our drink party. Mayank took out the bottles from his bag. Neel took out the snacks. The glasses were handed over to the individuals by Raghav. Mayank punched the three types of alcohol for everyone and prepared the servings. It seemed heaven when my Jonny Walker Black Label was punched with the vodka. The air from the window touching our body and the drink moving down our throat together took us to the clouds. It felt heavenly.

"What is going on here?" a voice came from a distance. We were not in a mood to listen to any one. But Rohan shouted aloud

"Oh God RPF (Railway Police Force)!!" as he said all of us looked up in a shock

"What is going on here?" the old cop repeated his statement.

"Nothing you old donkey, we are just having our drink" Neel shouted breaking all our expectations. She was drunk. Now she had lost control over her tongue. The old man got furious.

"What did you speak? I am going to penalize you for consuming alcohol in a public place" he said with terrible anger shaking his voice

"I said..." Neel was trying to repeat what she had said but Aditi pressed her lips with her hand. In the mean time Raghav moved out of his seat handing over his glass to me. He went close to the cop.

"Shut up Neel" a baffled soft spoken Sweety screamed. I could see Sweety giving a dirty look at Neel.

"Can we talk in private?" Raghav asked blinking one of his eyes. The cop hesitated but finally agreed. They had a long chat which was not at all audible to us in the distance. May be Raghav was bargaining on the bribe. I could only see a green coloured five hundred rupees which came out of Raghav's wallet and went into the pocket of the cop. Both of them came close to us.

"Okay do it fast and go to sleep without creating a mess" the cop said as his face clearly depicted that he was nerd who could never impress his wife.

"Yes sir, sure" Mayank replied and at the same time Neel threw up. Thank God she was near the window and all the stuff split outside the window. It was the most horrible part of the travel. Controlling her was the most difficult then. We decided to put her in her allotted berth. So, that she sleeps well before she could wake up all the passengers with her activities and noises.

It took us one more hour to complete our drink and then Mayank directed all the guys to reach the top floor i.e. the upper berth. He opened his laptop and we started watching the recently downloaded porn videos by him. He had all the latest porn movies that were uploaded in the internet. Any knowledge about porn needed then Mayank was the best source. All of us had a habit of taking free knowledge from him whenever we needed. The girls were now heavily drunk to go to sleep. We had a few hours of enjoyment on the upper berth. It was difficult to reach the berth after a considerable amount of alcohol consumption but we had somehow managed to reach there.

We decided to sleep after some of the newly uploaded south Indian MMS clips. I don't exactly remember the time or maybe I was heavily drunk even to look at my watch and find out the time. The next day I got up around 10.00 am when Mayank pushed me hard. My hangover was yet not gone. It feels good when you have just consumed alcohol but the worst part is when you came back to your senses. The hangover kills you. My head was badly aching due to the punch of alcohol prepared by Mayank. Everyone was in the same condition. Thanks to Sweety's head massage and Aditi's lemonade which relaxed me a lot. It's always good to have girls in your group because girls understand emotions and what you exactly need at the right time. Even though boys of my group were quiet understanding but girls are born sensitive and understanding.

We had some time for our arrival. So I went to the entrance of the train. I looked at the fast moving engine with a lot of smoke disrupting the atmosphere. I entangled my hand in the rods so that I don't fall out of the running train. I enjoyed the view of the North India. It looked lovely. The wind hitting me hard felt good. I thanked god for this beautiful day with those beautiful people around me, my friends. I didn't know what would happen to me without them. I would be all alone to myself if they had not come into my life. This reminded me about my childhood. I felt like crying but I said to myself "strong boys don't cry".

My Mom and Dad both worked for a social organization. They had regular international, national and rural visits. Fifteen to twenty days in a month they kept away from home. It had become difficult for me to watch them together. I kept complaining myself about this. When I was five years old my mom received a scholarship for her higher studies in Holland. So she had to leave for two years and I was left alone with my granny. Granny had become my best friend then. I visited my mom to Holland accompanied by my dad for a period of three months in between these two years. It was the best period in my life, not because I was in a European country but because I got full time from my parents. But as per the rule of the nature after a day then comes the night. My mom came back to India and the same routine continued and I kept on missing them both. After a few years I tried to stop complaining because I understood that they were working for me. They worked to give me a good education and a good standard of living. I started spending most of my time in my maternal grandfather's place. My grandfather became my friend, philosopher and guide. After I completed my tenth I meet all my group members who had somewhat the same sort of problems in their family. Although we had never sat down discussing family matters but we could understand each other really well. Then friends, alcohol and cigarettes became a part of my life or in fact they became my life. My friends became more important to me than my own life. I never felt lonely after that but somewhere deep in my heart an urge to spend time with my parents was killing me. I was already addicted spending most of the time all alone in my room. Loneliness became another good friend of mine or I can say it became my best friend.

* * * *

Chapter - 3

30th of March, 2009

We had reached the Jammu railway station a bit late in the morning. I was standing in close proximity to a book stall, my eyes searching for porn magazines. They fruitfully found some but I didn't have much gut to ask the shopkeeper for them. May be he would sue me away was my foremost fear. It was truly a teenage fear. I was thinking of the porn movies that we had seen last night in the train. This was one of the best entertainment teens could have in the train when they are together without the family members. Suddenly something hit me hard on my back. Though I did not turn to see what it was,

"Oh I am so sorry sir", a sweet voice said with a feeling of apology filled in it which forced me to turn back.

"That's ok ma'am", I said looking at the sweet girl tucking her hair behind her left ear. Her hand bag had hit me hard on my back.

She appeared to be a Punjabi girl with her long hair. She had attractive blue eyes. Her innocent looking blue eyes matched her white and blue salwar kameez. She was wearing a pair of blue gem ear rings. In other words she was looking like a typical appealing North Indian girl in pure blue. Her height was round about 5'3". She was fair enough to give the impression of being an angel. Her hands were as white as milk. Most importantly, her beauty had made me dumb. I kept looking at her even after her leaving the place. My eyes jammed with the beautiful angel as if someone had pasted them with glue. I used my dexterous wits to plan a trap on this beauty queen.

My companions warned me of the girl's strict looking father whom I thought would have just retired from Hitler's army. He unquestionably looked strict with big glasses fit into his lizard coloured frame and a well built body. How could this person have such a beautiful daughter? Is it possible? Or maybe she was not his daughter. Anything was possible. I had many such questions in my mind. The person was a north Indian personality who looked more like a south Indian or a tollywood villain. But I did not care much about this; I wanted the girl at any cost. She had stolen away my heart with her first glance.

"Gyan be careful before you do something", Neel warned

"He's going to kill you if he knows that you are after her daughter", Mayank exclaimed, his voice cracking with a terrified expression, as if someone had slapped him for improper use of the washroom.

"Don't worry guys and how do you know that she is his daughter?" I said. My feet had started following the angry old man before I could complete my statement.

"What are you doing man? He is not going to spare you even if he gets a hint about your thoughts. He looks really dodgy............." Rohan shouted which I think maximum of the passengers standing on the platform of the Jammu station must have heard.

"Just fuck off man", I shouted at him looking into his eyes just to shut his incorrigible mouth.

By this time the station superintendent had smelt something fishy going on around. I could see him keeping an eye on the group which did not bother me much. I was bothered more concerning the beauty queen. I followed the girl's father. He went to the prepaid taxi stand from where he booked a Pajero for the family to Hotel Green Valley, Srinagar. *"Ohh fuck man, it's the same hotel we had booked"* I thought and was going to speak it out but I controlled my tongue to keep myself on a safer side. *"No slangs dude if you do not want to lose her before you get her",* I said to myself. We had booked two rooms in the same hotel through the internet with a lot of difficulties, as all of us were new to these types of booking. I reserved a non AC Tata sumo which cost me much less than the north Indians Pajero. I didn't think there was any use of an AC car in place where there is snow fall. We had a lot of fun in the car on our way to Srinagar which was a very long travel of about 12 hours. But my mind was still stuck with the sweet beautiful blue eyes of the north Indian girl.

After a long exhausting journey we finally reached the hotel in the evening. I went straight to the manager who welcomed us with a welcome drink. I enquired about the north Indian family even before I could complete my drink. My brain had already commenced outlining the agenda.

"Dude can you provide us rooms near the north Indians, who just arrived in a Pajero" I asked the manager. I used the word North Indians, as I had a cent percent confirmation that they were not anywhere from the south, because their colour and accent of speaking was enough to show the fact.

"Sir, they are the Chittra's from Rajasthan, but why do you need a room near theirs?" manager enquired with a hint of surprise. I was completely wrong with my guess of the girl being a Punjabi girl. She was a Rajasthani princess.

"Try to understand dude it's a case of a stolen heart." Mayank prompted with the others giggling around him like cartoon characters. And I hated Mayank for his wild and unruly way of expressing things.

The manager instantly understood Mayank's indication. He started flipping all the way through his register to locate if there were any unoccupied rooms near the room of the Chittra family. As soon as he found the vacancy he handed over the keys of the rooms which were just besides the rooms of the royals of Rajasthan.

"That's really great of you sir", I said looking at the manager with a grateful look and climbed up the stairs to our room.

All of us were tired enough to get hold of the bed and excited enough to get up early and move out for sightseeing. But my thoughts were still hanging around the sweet little blue eyes and the pink succulent lips of the young beautiful angel. She had now become a challenge for me. I named her mission Rajasthan.

The Rajasthani family had four members in their group which included the Hitler's retired army personnel i.e the father (Mr. Chittra), the mother (Mrs. Chittra) and their two young charming and beautiful princesses Salini and Minti. There was confusion with these two names (ohh man…… Is it Salini or Minti?). The name of the heart stealer was not yet identified. Mr.Chittra was working with a public sector bank in Jaipur, Rajasthan. They were probably having a family holiday after their daughters' final examinations. This information was provided to me by the hot and sexy receptionist on the ground floor of the hotel after a bribe of three hundred bucks!! And most importantly a flying kiss to which I thought I would be slapped but instead she gave an accepting expression. After all I was a stud!!!

* * * *

Chapter - 4

31st of March, 2009

"Get up stupid creatures", a voice came from outside the door

The door was banged with such a velocity that I thought if it was not opened within a short notice then it was going to be broken down. I ran down to the door to open it in my half sleep mode. It was Neel with a jug in her hand. I really did not have much idea about what she was doing with a jug full of water in her hand. May be she had found a part time job of a waitress!! It was the first thought which came into my sleepy mind. She pushed my half alert and half sleepy body away from her way and dashed into the room.

"What the hell are you doing? It is already 7.30", she shouted almost disturbing the other guests of the hotel.

"We are in the heaven of sleep", a reluctant voice came from under the blanket

She jumped on the bed like a short heighted monkey. Now I think I had got the idea about the jug as well as the water in it. She dropped all the water in the jug on all the sleepy morons. Thank God I had moved out to open the door.

"Yeah, don't…" I said but it was so late by now. The soft cottons of the bed had virtually absorbed almost two litres of water.

"Get up you lazy buffaloes." Neel shouted and this time with a louder intensity.

"Ohhhh please fuck off and get lost from here immediately, idiot", Raghav shouted back at her. She didn't have any reaction to his statement except a wry and stupid smile to which I always had an aversion. She had become well acquainted with the filthy words of Raghav by now, so she didn't have much to speak.

"Get ready and get to the breakfast table by 8.00", she commanded and went out of the room as a commander of the national cadet cop.

It took us only twenty odd minutes to get ready and reach the table as obedient school going young kids of Neel, before she could fire back at us again with a jug full of water. None of us had taken a bath due to the extreme cold condition of Kashmir. Our bodies were too chilled to come in touch with water. The Rajasthani clan was already present in the restaurant having their breakfast. I could see some south Indian breakfast i.e idli and chutney on their table. I was stunned to watch north Indians having south Indian breakfast in the northern most part of the country.

It was the first time when I had a direct eye contact with my sweetheart in the restaurant. I could not concentrate much on my favourite puri and sabji. Most of my concentration was attracted by the Rajasthani family. I could see Mrs. Chittra looking so young. I could never imagine her getting married to Mr. Chittra on her own will. May be she was kidnapped and forcefully married to Mr. Chittra was my first look thought.

"Ohh God, how did this happen?" Mr. Chittra was busy over his phone with terrified expressions, which he usually had since I had seen him. But this time I could feel a more intense one.

"But is it that we are going to waste the day just in the hotel room", he continued. And now I was interested in knowing what was going on.

Our Tata sumo was already parked in the hotel campus for our visit to Sonemargh. I got a hint of problem going on in the Rajasthan base camp. My dexterous brain started working faster than the speed of light. I went straight to the manger and asked what was going on.

"I exactly do not know sir but I think the car which was going to pick them up for Gulmarg visit has faced an accident somewhere." Manager said

"Wow that's great…" I said as the manager looked at me as if I had kissed their hotel's receptionist in front of him.

"Yeah, can you do something for me?" I asked looking straight into the eyes of the manager without a blink of my eye.

"What sir?" he asked politely as a puppet

"Go and ask the family if they had any problem joining us to Sonemargh instead of wasting the whole day in the hotel room." I said as the time had come for the execution of my planned agenda.

"What the fuck are you doing!!" Aditi shouted

"Just shut up and stand by the side." Mayank said supporting me

I had never expected Mayank supporting me but it was just amazing. The manager was confused and gave me innocent looks. May be he was puzzled or may be shocked to hear a girl speaking out slangs. Or the worst case may be that he was afraid of going to the tollywood villain. Mr. Chittra was in fact looking more dangerous now. Mayank slid a hundred rupees note into the manager's waist coat pocket which seemed dirty but that had worked. We were good at bribing people. He walked away like a brave lion as soon as he felt the sensation of the hundred rupees note in his pocket. Money does anything that looks impossible, at least in India.

"Salini come here fast", Mrs. Chittra called for her daughter

It was my angel named Salini. My angel was playing with the fury puppies of Srinagar. I had finally got to know the name of my sweetheart. Mayank seemed more excited than me when he heard that.

"Hey!! Yours is Salini and mine is Minti!!" Mayank exclaimed with excitement filled in his voice.

"What the hell???" I asked with a shocking expression

"I meant your girl's name is Salini." Mayank said trying to hide his face. Hiding of face didn't work as he knew he had already released his stupidity.

"What do you mean by my girl, idiot" I said. And he preferred to keep his mouth shut.

He understood that I had fathomed his feelings for Minti. Then I came to know why he had supported me to convince the manager to go to Mr. Chittra and talk about the sharing of the taxi. In the mean time the manager had arranged a meeting with Mr. Ranveer Chittra, my angel's father.

"Hi, Mr. Ranveer", I said with a hint of innocence in my voice

"Hello beta", he said. He spoke these words so softly that I felt guilty of calling him a tollywood villain and retired army personnel of Hitler's army.

He was a sweet person but was a reserved personality which could have put my plans to danger and my mission Rajasthan could have failed. But my quick-witted brain was running faster than the Rajdhani Express influencing upon him. I asked him to come with us but had to face many of his queries. I had never ever used so much brain even to write my papers in the examination halls.

"Let's go dad." Salini said

"Come on sir, do not think much. Let's have fun together." I said taking her side. The last four words I spoke were just for Salini and no one else. *Fuck off man why do you old people think so much before taking any decision. And if your answer is no to my invitation then I would not be guilty for calling you a tollywood villain.* I thought. But finally I could comfortably breathe air into my lungs when he agreed to my suggestion.

"God, I can't walk anymore", Mrs. Chittra said

"Don't worry maam we have already walked half the distance", Rohan said

"And another half left", Neel expressed arrogantly as if someone had forced her to jump from the hill we were walking on. She never wanted outsiders to join us for the trip.

"I can't walk anymore, please", Mrs. Chittra scoffed

We had reached Sonemargh but had to park our taxi a kilometre back behind the snow area and climb up the hill from there. Mr. and Mrs. Chittra decided to halt back on the half way but their daughters were excited enough to play with the snow. So they accompanied us.

"Okay you old couples you enjoy your date and let us enjoy ours", Mayank whispered into my ears

"Shut up idiot, you are going to kill me someday", I shouted back at him attracting the attention of both the Rajasthani girls. But I don't think they would have heard our conversation.

It was a good chance for us to know each other. I had been a killer in my past commencing an interaction with any girl but I didn't know why I fumbled starting up a conversation with Salini. I thought it would be good to start the discourse with Minti rather than Salini although we had already spent 20 minutes together but I was not able the start an interaction with her. *Come on Gyan you have a killer in you. You can do it* I spoke to myself. Then finally after having a light talk with Minti I started to have a chat with my mission Rajasthan.

She responded well to our first conversation. She had just taken admission for her junior college and her elder sister had taken her final exams for the junior college. And most importantly she never had a boyfriend. Salu was a cute childish girl with positivity glazing out from her face. She was a very loving and caring personality. I could not resist myself from loving her. Her beautiful cute blue eyes were deep enough for me to drown in them. Her silky black hair was shinning bright as I could see the sun's rays reflecting after touching them. I was envious of the sun for touching her. Her lips were very attractive. The pink colour of her lips had blown my sense away into the heaven. She had started liking my company and her lips were forcing me to kiss them. I had to resist myself considering the fact of huge audience and her elder sister, even though I had been a close friend of her elder sister. But none of a close friend would ever allow me to kiss her younger sister neither in public nor in any private place.

It was the most romantic moment when we started playing with the snowball. Some of the snowballs thrown from her were mis targeted to my face, which really hurt me. But I did not have much gut to reveal them or maybe I did not want her to feel guilty for hurting me. One of my mis targeted shots allowed me to take her into my arms for the first time. Those lovely moments will never bolt out of my head.

"This is unfair", Neel complained.

"What's not fair", Rohan enquired

"A five buck packet noodles is prepared and sold at hundred bucks!!!!!!!" Neel said with such dumb expression as if someone had bankrupted her Swiss bank account.

"Just shut up idiot and have your noodles", Mayank said

"You are never going to change dumbo", Rohan said looking at Neel and nodding his head.

"Noooo…" she said with a huge smile emancipating her ludicrousness.

We were on the snow and enjoying the snow under our gumboots. Moreover we were trying to recover from frost bite. It wasn't one but we felt as if we had faced one after our snowball fight. Salini and I had become good and close friends though Mayank could not do much with Minti because she already had a boyfriend.

* * * *

"Can I have some more Sahi Paneer please?" Salini asked

"Ya sure ma'am", I said as I passed the bowl to her hand just sitting next to her. But the word 'ma'am' used here was not at all same as the one which was used at the Jammu railway station when we had first faced each other. This was a sarcastic one which I was now using to tease her reminding her about the station.

"Kashmiri kofta is really amazing, isn't it?" Neel said

"You have said something sensible after years, Neel", Rohan said just looking at his plate and thoroughly enjoying his food.

"I always speak sensibly but you need to have a brain to understand them." Neel fought back

"I…" Rohan tried to continue but Mayank stopped him

"Cut the crap both of you and have your dinner", Mayank spoke

Mayank thought he was sensible enough to attract the attention of all the members on the table as I could see a proud smile on his face. The smile looked crackbrained to me. Anyways that was not vital for me, but what was important was that Mr. Chittra had invited us for sharing the dinner table. And her younger daughter getting closer to me or may be something else. Salini and I were playing the game of footsie under the table which gave me a positive hint towards our relationship. After dinner we had a long chat with the Chittra's. My dexterous devil brain had been doing its work. Throughout the chat my hand was crossed with Salini's under the table giving me a sensation of love. Even though she wanted to free her hands in between I never allowed her to do it. I would just look at her with a smile on my face. Of course we could not have our hands crossed in front of everybody as I knew the result of doing that. And I did not want to lose her so early. I wanted to kiss her at that moment as her lips were driving me crazy. But I had to resist my uncontrollable feelings as I knew it would be a blunder in presence of the senior Chittra's and Salini's elder sister.

"Why don't we move together tomorrow morning to Gulmarg?" I said looking at Mr. Chittra and using my sharp witted brain. I knew I took him by surprise. That's the best way to give heart attacks to the oldies to which they can never say a "NO" at a glance. If I had used even a single percent of my brain of what I was using then into my studies I would have been the topper of my college. But I preferred using it in other productive ways!!

"Yes dad it's a brilliant idea", Salini spoke in my support. It brought a monumental smile on my face impulsively.

"Dad we are really enjoying with them" Minti said giving a smile and then turning to Mayank to my utter surprise. Was she trying to flirt with Mayank?

We had a long discussion about the visit to Gulmarg next morning. The tollywood villain gave some odd expressions as if I had asked him to jump from the top floor of the hotel building. But finally the positive word came out from the oldy. I had my fingers crossed throughout the slow process of his decision making. *"I would have punched you old man if you would have tried to play the role of a villain in my love life."* I spoke to myself.

"Stupid oldy has put his daughter into danger", Mayank whispered into my ears.

This time I did not tell anything. May be I was not able to tell anything with my heart filled with extreme amount of joy. Salini was also very happy. Her face seemed to have hid the brightest moonlight evening of the month. Finally my dexterous brain had prevailed over Mr. Chittra.

After some heavy and flavoursome Kashmiri food we wished each other goodnight and moved towards our room. The only problem I faced the whole night was sleeplessness. Salini's thoughts were wandering throughout my heart and mind as if she had captured both of them. May be the same thing was happening in the room next to ours. I had somehow made up my mind to propose to her for being my girlfriend. *Have I fallen into the ditch of love? Is it possible for a killer like me to have a girlfriend that too from Rajasthan? Can it happen so soon or was it just an attraction? Can I propose to her? Will she accept my proposal?* So many thoughts were going through my astute brain which had become a helpless lover at this moment of time. *Fuck off man, just shut your eyes and sleep* I said to myself but could not capture my thoughts moving outside the room to the room beside ours.

* * * *

Chapter - 5

1st of April, 2009

"Where is the snow? Why is it called the mini Switzerland? What are we waiting for? Bla bla bla…" Aditi questioned as if she had put all the doubts of her Geography lectures straight away.

"Stop…" Neel interrupted her

"We have to take a cable car to reach the snow", Rohan answered

"And rest of your questions will be answered when you reach the snow", Neel said

"Can you please get eleven tickets", I said looking at Mayank.

He looked at me with a horrible expression as if I had asked him to sign a porn movie as the lead role. He actually did not want to move away from Minti. Then I looked at Rohan with unimpeachable eyes and my eyes asked for a favour. I didn't want to separate Salini from me even for a second. Rohan was sharp enough to understand my directions. We soon had the tickets in our hand and proceeded towards the cable car. When we reached the hill top we still had to walk a long distance to reach the snow.

"Oh God can't walk anymore", Mrs. Chittra said

"Ohh yes thank God and thank you Mrs. Chittra I was just waiting for the same statement since so long." I spoke to myself. I wanted to jump around on the hill but had to give the false expression of being very sad that Mrs. Chittra would not be able to come up with us.

"Salini and Minti, Do you want to go up there?" Mr. Chittra asked

"Yes dad" both replied as identical twins react to situations

"Please come back soon", Mr. Chittra requested

"Sure uncle we will be back within an hour or two", I prompted happily

We used our full strength to reach the top near the snow. I was very excited to spend some lone time with Salu and to propose to her as I had decided the previous night. I was exhausted on reaching the snow but Salu's presence had taken away all my exertion. As soon as we reached the snow, I went down on my knees holding her hand and pulling out a blood red rose from my pocket.

"I love you..." I said

On the other hand I was very nervous of losing her friendship. The first finger of my left hand was resting over the second waiting for a reply. Salini's reactions were to be marked by the viewer. She had never expected this to happen so early. I am sure she knew that this is going to happen someday or the other. The first smile gave me a positive reaction which brought some relief to my heart. I was waiting for those three magical words. Halting for few seconds, with a bit of shyness on her face and a sweet blush which made her look the most beautiful girl on the world,

"I love you too", she replied.

I had gone mad for a moment, running and jumping on the snow. The beauty spot on her face made her look prettier. My mission Rajasthan was successful. It was first of April. I first doubted if she was making a fool of me on the April fool day but it was nothing like that. She actually meant it and I can never forget the date. There was no limit to my joviality. My eyes were filled with tears of exuberance. Of course she was my first love. And most significantly the first love of a killer who only believed in flirting but not making girlfriends. She had struck the killer down. I hugged her and repeated those to make her feel comfortable. My group was more excited than me. Not because I was committed to someone but because we were going to celebrate it with a party. Though we could not have a romantic candle light dinner but we managed to have an open sunlight lunch on the snow. I think it was the most amazing and romantic date on the mini Switzerland I have ever had with any other girl.

The time was running away fast. Minti and I had become good friends now. And even Salini was very close to her. So, it was not a big deal for us to share everything with her. In fact both the sisters had become a part of the group by now. The same night we had a long chat till the midnight in the junior Chittra's room.

* * * *

Chapter - 6

2nd of April, 2009

"We need a doctor", Mayank said running to the manager

"Why??????" I asked in a shock as I had no idea about what was going on.

"Aunty is suffering from serious fever", Mayank said

"Who is aunty now????" I asked as a fool

"Stupid, your estimated mother in law", He answered but with anger filled in his voice. I had always addressed her as Mrs. Chittra. And the word "estimated" without any doubt sounded odd at the situation. But Mayank always had a habit of saying stupid things at serious times.

The doctor soon arrived in the room. He was also a tourist to Kashmir residing in the same hotel. Doctors take an oath that they would not tell no to any patient. So, he was an honest doctor to help us out. He prescribed some medicines which Raghav brought from a nearby medicine store. But Mrs. Chittra's health was still retrogressing. Mr. Ranveer had to stay back with his wife to support her. He permitted Salini and Minti to visit Pahelgam with us. It was the first time I had taken Mr. Ranveer's name with so much respect since the time I had witnessed him.

It was a beautiful and fanciful place. But Salini's agitated spirit did not let me enjoy the day. However I managed to alleviate both the sisters and bring their spirits up. We travelled to some of the retail outlets to squeal on some of the kashmiri products for our families and relatives. I presented a beautiful pure white salwar suit to my warm hearted would be mistress. I asked her to wear it when she comes down to Bhubaneswar, my hometown in Odisha. We planned a long ride on my bike all through the city. She was really excited at my gesture. Salu sent an elegant green salwar suit for my mom which was appreciated by mom, though I had never discussed anything about Salu with her.

After doing a plentiful of shopping the five girls of the group including Salini and Minti returned to the restaurant. The vexed boys including me were waiting for them for about an hour. Salu managed to overcome my provocation with an amiable kiss before I could explode on anyone. Minti vanquished Mayank's fret with a winsome smile. And the rest of the guys had to keep their mouths shut. We took our lunch which was something different named Pakis Paneer biriyani. It was really difficult for me to bear the taste of the dish but I engulfed it due to unbearable hunger.

We had to travel back about hundred and twenty kilometres to reach the hotel. The tollywood villain and his sweet sick wife would be waiting for us. The driver was hurrying us up as it was getting late. The fear of a terrorist attack was psychologically killing him. He was behaving as if he had to urgently use the toilet which was only available in the hotel Green Valley. Though the day was not very exciting and optimistic for us but we enjoyed each other's company. Nothing could put me into boredom till I had the companionship of my sweet baby, Salu. We reached the hotel at 9.00 in the evening. I could see the stress on Mr. Chittra's face when we entered the hotel. But I could even feel the sensation of faith in the group in his voice when we had a light talk just after the return in the reception hall of the hotel.

"Wow aunty you are fit now." Aditi echoed

"Yes beta", Mrs. Chittra said with a friendly gesture depicting more faith in us.

Mayank gave Mrs. Chittra a head massage to flatter her for her elder sister, which I think gave her a huge relief. *But sorry dude you can't have your hand on Minti. She was already having a boyfriend,* I thought. With all the fun going on the time passed and the fourth day was on the verge of leaving us.

* * * *

Chapter - 7

3rd of April, 2009

"Prince it's our last day", Salu said with her hands on mine and her head resting on my shoulder. She had started addressing me as Prince instead of Gyan and I loved it.

"Yes baby", I said with a bit of depressed voice

"Will you come to Rajasthan to meet me?" She asked

"Sure my sweet Angel, but there is a condition", I said

"What condition now???" She asked with a surprise

"The condition is that you are not going to get upset today", I said

She just tried to smile. But I knew she was upset. She didn't want to leave me and go. I knew it was our last day in Kashmir. I was even low spirited but I tried to keep myself cool and hide my emotions.

Guess what!!!!! We were on the Dal Lake in the boat house. The rest of the people had gone to explore the Dal Lake on the Shikara (a small boat kind of thing) including the senior Chittra's. After the group returned from their expedition we decided not to have long travels, instead to go on for sightseeing of the Srinagar city to avoid exhausting ourselves. We also had to do some shopping for our families and relatives.

We visited the Mughal gardens which were very beautiful and optimistic. Those gardens were very clean and well maintained unlike some of the uncared gardens of India. Some photo shoots in the garden delayed our proceedings. Neel was almost making her portfolio in the garden as if she was very soon going to sign a modelling contract. I was getting frustrated. I would have smashed her if the Rajasthani family wasn't travelling with us. My restlessness was increasing as the time passed because I was not able to spend time with my sweet baby. Minti's eye caught my tossing and turning. She immediately turned to me and fired me a question about my roving nature. I just gave a smile and moved away from the place thinking that Mr. Chittra might mark my behaviour. And I didn't like being caught red handed.

After a long photo shoot, we moved towards the market for shopping. Finally, after an extensive wait I got a chance to while away my time with Salu. Minti had planned and put us a hundred meters back so that we could spend a quality time with each other. I really wanted to kiss Minti for what she had done for me. But practically I could not do it because she was my sweetheart's sister.

Everything was going on peacefully when suddenly a strike opened up. As per the shopkeepers the strike was due to the dead body of a young lad found from the dustbin. Salu and I could not match up with the group. It was literally a breakneck move of the internal war between the public and the armed forces. We were pulled into a garment shop by some obliging shopkeepers. They told us that it was risky moving out till the situation had cooled down. The same situation was there with the group but I was really tensed about my friends' safety. The most difficult situation was that the group had four girls and a lady included in it. Salu was also very unease about her parents and her sister. The people of Kashmir were very friendly. They lent a helping hand to the tourists to safeguard them from any problem which would bring a negative aspect about the state.

Those hours became the most treasure time for us to share our feelings and love for each other. I was happy to share my family culture with her to make her feel a bit more comfortable with me. We shared our likings and dislikes. Our gestures were of the true lovers and not of the hoaxed ones. Slowly we started addressing each other as "JAAN" which meant life. It was in fact true. We had become each other's life in such a short span of life. I tried my best diverting her attention from the war outside but somewhere deep in her heart she was very worried about her sister and parents.

On the other hand the internal war was still on a rage on the other side of the closed shutter. I was thrilled to watch what was happening on behind the shutter. In fact it is truly said hot blood is always desperate for something which looks dangerous and adventurous. Salu's hesitance and plead could not stop me from moving out. I was also very worried about my friends and their security. I even had to inform them that everything was well and good and they need not worry about us.

The moment I marched out, my eyes were blinded for a couple of minutes. I could catch the sight of blood sheds all over the road. I could glimpse at the dead bodies fallen on the midway. I espied the people killing each other. The helpless armed forces were just the audience to the uncontrollable mob. I had only viewed such dangerous situations in movies. But now, my eyes could see something like that in real life. The huge tyres burning on the road had blocked the path for any conveyance to pass through them. People were shouting at each other with venom filled in their heart and mouth. As per the army personnel the problem was created by the venal politicians who valued hard cash more than the lives of their people. When the situation went out of control from the hands of the land forces, they opened up seize fire on the general public. Including some felons many innocent individuals lost their precious lives in front of my eyes. Apart from the civilians, the bodies of the infantries were teetering on the ground. My mind was in a melancholic state. My eyes were filled. I was guilty for not doing anything to stop the useless fights which had no outcome. But I could only be a mere helpless viewer to the milieu.

Are we the citizens of a secular country? If yes, why do we fight in the name of religion, caste and creed? Can we stop fighting with each other? Can we become a developed country instead of being called a developing country since six decades of our independence? Can we love peace instead of violence? These questions including many others came up in my mind, but there was no one to answer them.

There was a lot of risk and I had to save myself from those huge rocks and bullets fired. But I managed to locate the group and inform them that Salini was ok and they should not worry about our security. Mayank and Minti accompanied me to the shop where Salini was desperately waiting for me. It took us more than half an hour to cover a distance of less than a hundred meters. Finally with a lot of hotchpotch we managed to reach the place where Salu was waiting for us.

She rushed and hugged me tight with tears rolling down her eyes as if I had just returned from the kargil war. She was worried about my surveillance since I had moved out. I was a bit conscious due to the presence of Mayank, Minti and rest of the audience who were looking at us as if some bollywood movie was being shot. Trying to console my sweetheart,

"Hey what happened to my brave girl", I said with my fingers busy removing drops of tear from her sweet face.

"Prince, you are mine and I can't lose you at any cost", she said with tears still running down her eyes

It was now difficult controlling her emotions. I hugged her ignoring the world around me. I did not care for the presence of Minti. This had brought tears in her eyes. First time the killer was not able to tolerate tears in a girl's eyes. Was it love? I did not have much idea about this. I had never even thought of falling in love with someone.

To take us out of our emotional breakdown condition Mayank cracked a few jokes followed by some of his stupid questions,

"When are you both getting married?" Mayank asked,

"Stupid, it's just five days we have met" I said,

"So what is the problem?" He asked like a stupid and I felt like bashing his head with a stone as I had no interest in answering his question.

"Don't worry Mayank bhaiya we are going to invite you for our marriage party" Salu said with a smile on her face.

After this reply Mayank had become a laughing stock for all of us. But thank God, this had helped me taking out Salini from her emotional trauma. We went to the extreme left corner of the shop to continue our chat. Mayank took a chance to flirt with Minti, even though he knew about the fact that Minti had a boyfriend.

It was almost 4.00 in the evening and the disturbed surroundings outside the shutter were cooling down. The groups were getting ready to move out towards the hotel. It was becoming the most difficult situation for me to part from my beloved. The sun was setting. We moved towards the hotel chatting with each other about various cultures followed in our own states i.e Odisha and Rajasthan. Mrs. Chittra told us about the culture of marriage which went on for more than seven days in every family. It was almost like attending an hour of physics lecture without practical classes. It became a tremendous boredom for rest of the lot including Salini. It had havocked all the organs of the nervous system of my group members. But I was too much interested to the harangue. I thought it would be very helpful for me increasing the compatibility between Salu and me. During this session, Salu must have pinched me a thousand times with beautiful smiles on her face depicting shyness in them. She had probably started thinking of her marriage days. She was absent minded throughout the walk to the hotel thinking about me and may be our combined future. Whenever I tried to talk to her,

"Chup, ssssshhhhhhhhhhh..., don't disturb me I am thinking about something important", she said with a smile on her face which made her look like an angel. I never understood what was so important when you are just out of such a terrified atmosphere.

"Paneer Kofta is brilliant", Sweety said

"We are famous for this dish all over Srinagar, madam", the waiter serving us immediately replied

"Even the biriyani is pretty good", Mrs. Chittra said

"Thank you ma'am", he said with pride as if he was receiving Oscar

I was dumb as it was very difficult to tolerate the pain of partition. Neither Salu nor I could express our feelings due to the presence of her parents. We had to give fake smiles to show that we were enjoying our dinner on the table. It was very difficult for me to even swallow a single bite of my favourite masala kulcha and paneer kofta. *Fuck man I am ready to give away anything if someone could help us not getting parted, but I knew it well that the tollywood villain is going to kill me if I asked for something like that.* My sub-conscious mind wanted to tell but the conscious one didn't permit me. We managed to complete our dinner with a lot of difficulties. I had seen Minti looking at me with suspicious looks. I think she had also marked the doleful looks of her sister.

We had a long conversation in our room including Minti and Salu after the senior Chittra's went to sleep.

"Salu and the thief of my sister's heart, please follow me", Minti said with a grave and serious voice.

"Why?" I asked with a shock. I was afraid if she was going to take us to her parents and tell them about our love story.

"No questions please", She answered

And we followed her, as school students being taken out of the classroom to be punished by an old strict headmaster. She took both of us to their room. And on the door she declared that she had decided to let us a few moments of private talk. As soon as I heard this I was overwhelmed. Salu jumped at her kissing her all over her face completely ignoring my presence. But I was jealous. I actually wanted those.

"It's ok now, no need to butter me more, go and have a peaceful chat for the next one hour", She said looking at Salu

"Thank you my sweet sis", Salu said

"Just chat and nothing else", she said sarcastically

I am sure Salu understood it and it had also struck my dexterous brain. She had put a banner of **BE CAREFULL!!!!** And **NO SEX!!!!** Though I had no such intensions planned in my mind.

"Don't you think I also deserved some of those sweet kisses", I said as we were entering the room

The moment I spoke those words she ran to the bed and hid her face with a pillow fallen on the top right corner of the bed. I proceeded towards her, held her hand, pulled her into my arms and gave a soothing kiss on her forehead. It became the most romantic moment we had ever spent with each other. Though we were just given a time of an hour by Minti, it was enough for both of us to speak our heart out to each other. Salu lying down on my arms with her head resting on my shoulder and her fingers crossed with mine, I felt as if I was floating on the clouds. It was the happiest situation ever faced in life for both of us as we tasted the succulent flavour of our first love. I brought my face close to her with one hand resting on her waist and the other on my angel's soft cheeks. My lips went close to the attractive, pink and sappy lips of my sweet heart. Within no time they touched each other and I faced the most amorous phase of my life. My hands still resting on her waist and my lips rolling down her neck had passed a high voltage current in both of us. Both of us were lying down in each other's arm with our eyes closed. The only light which was switched on was the bed lamp next to the bed. The dim light of the bed lamp made the ambience more romantic. It was really nice of Minti to give us our own space and to enjoy passionately. But when I looked at my sweet heart I could see a little kid with some faint hearted eye. I could easily make out the reason of the diffident milieu. I went close to her taking her into my arms and embracing her tight.

"Baby I won't do any such thing for which both of us have to repent in future, and you may be questioned by the outsiders", I said moving my lips close to her ear.

This statement from me made her so free from hardship that I could see a colossal smile coming followed by few droplets of tears rolling down her beautiful cheeks. Her eyes showed increment in faith for me. I could not tolerate my darling weeping. So I enfolded her tightly in my arms giving her warmth of loyalty and care. Both of us lying on the bed with our hearts entangled with each other and most importantly a very strong bond of love and faith created between us.

"Please baby never let me alone", Salu said

"Don't worry my dear angel I won't let you go even if the condition is the worst", I said with the power of promise filled in it

"Is it?" she asked sarcastically,

"Any doubt?" I asked in return,

"No doubts on my prince", she said with an angel's smile

Our beautiful colloquy was on but soon it was disturbed by the ring of the telephone. I would have smashed the telephone or may be the inventor to invent it and disturb us in our romantic chat. My angel took the call. I could not take the call with a fear of the senior Chittra's. The phone was on loudspeaker. It was Minti. I was relaxed listening to Minti's voice.

"Madam is it over?" Minti asked and I could hear the roar from the other side by the group.

What do you mean by is it over? And what do you expect to get over after putting a huge restriction placard around my neck of NO SEX!!!!!

"Yes di almost", Salu said

"Can we have a chat in the group?" Minti asked

"Yes we will be there in next five minutes", I prompted

She actually wanted to spend some more time with me. I also wanted the same but had to move out before I was thrashed by Minti. With a lot of hesitance Salu agreed to move towards the group completely against her will. Just as we were moving out of the room,

"I love you Prince and you must know that you are mine and I will never let you go." She said

"I love you too my sweet baby and I know it well", I said as a kid

Her hand on my shoulder and the other hand bringing me near her to rest her head on my chest.

"Baby when you take me into your arms and I rest peacefully on your chest it gives me the highest gratification I have ever had in my life." She said and I was speechless

May be we were not as mature as Romeo and Juliet or the other popular lovers of society but our love was mature and may be as matured as the great lovers of the present civilization. We lived for each other now. Every moment my thoughts were embraced by her. And obviously the vice versa was cent percent true. I always thought how god could be so grateful to me to give me such a nice and caring personality so early in my life. I always prayed the almighty to keep my sweetheart happy and out of problems.

After an hour of sweet and passionate private talk we moved to the group. We were welcomed with deceptive smiles and various abrupt noises, which probably had disturbed the people staying close to the room. I wanted to tell them *Guys please do not get over excited and please do not panic.*

I am still a virgin as there was a restriction banner of NO SEX!!!! Most importantly I did not want to hurt my baby. But I thought it was not at all advisable to speak those words in Minti's presence. Even though she had become very close to each and every member of the group, it wouldn't be sensible.

The party started with snacks, cold drinks, beer and some hard drinks for studs like us. Neel was over thrilled looking at the drinks. We had not had any, since the day we were in Kashmir. I was about to take a sip of my hard peg when a hand became an obstruction close to my lips. Who else could it be? The obvious answer was Salu.

"Sir, from this moment you have to promise me that you will not take any harmful drinks", she said

"Come on baby a single peg is not going to harm me", I protested

"A single peg!!!!!!", she exclaimed with anger as if she is going to thrash me.

"Please dear", I continued my protest in a sweet manner

"I won't allow you a single sip from this glass, and stop dreaming about a full peg", she spoke and simultaneously snatched away the glass from my hand and handed me a glass of cold drinks.

"Now you can drink a full peg in fact two more are also allowed", she said as I was struck dumb to the situation

"Cheers baby", Neel prompted with an intension of teasing me

"That's the demerit of having a girlfriend", a voice came from the right corner of the room. It was Mayank. He was having a good time with his glass of whisky lying down on the sofa. He also relished pulling my leg. I was jealous. I was feeling as if someone had snatched a kid's Cadbury dairy milk and handed him a lolly pop instead of that. Minti threw a pillow on Mayank protesting his statement. I could see a bit of uneasy feeling in Salu's eyes to this statement. I took her in my arms and drank the full glass of cold drink in one shot to ease her. Then a shy smile from Salu relaxed me. As soon as she came out of her confused state she took my hand over her head with a jerk. It was amazingly shocking for me as well as the other members of the room.

"Swear on me that you will never drink till I am there with you", she said

"What do you mean by till you are there with me?" I opposed as I was trying to divert the topic. I didn't want to stop boozing with my friends!!! The party always feels incomplete without hard drinks.

"Sorry I meant forever", she said with her hands still over my head as I tried to remove it. She was destroying my hair style!!

"That's like a good girl", I prompted and thought she would have forgotten about the promise.

"Come on I want you to promise me now" She said and I realized how wrong my thoughts were

"I promise", I continued with a sad face.

"Then what are we going to do with the Jonny Walker Black Label" Rohan asked scratching his head and Salu gave him a dirty look. No words could fit into the situation from me so I decided to shut up and keep myself on the safer side.

I really felt the pain of promising her to stop drinking. I wanted to tell her a big no. But her innocent face made me do whatever it wanted me to do. Now I could only have cold drinks in pubs, discos and parties. I could not compete with friends in my tequila shots in the discos. I could not even touch glasses which contained alcohol. I could only see them from a distance drunk by my friends. But I really did not mind these small things if I had my Salu's love with me. I kept the stick of the lolly pop (i.e. the empty glass of cold drinks) down to kiss her. Suddenly Mayank poked his nose before I could kiss her.

"Salu, he doesn't only drink but also has a bad habit of smoking", Mayank said with a voice of a drunkard and took a stroke into his mouth from his burning cigarette.

I would have smashed his head with the empty bottle of whisky fallen in front of me, if Salu and Minti were not there in the room. I really didn't know whether he had lost his marbles or someone had struck him hard on his back. The sweet angry girl whom I had cooled down just before few minutes charged at me again, but this time with a very soft voice.

"Is it Prince? Do you smoke?" she fired her question,

I could not lie to her innocent face and beautiful blue and confused eyes which demanded an immediate answer from me. I knew she wanted to listen to a negative response but the case was not that. I wished I wouldn't have smoked in my past. But it is truly said if wishes were horses then beggars would ride.

"Yes..." I said with a pause and lot of hesitation,

"You……." She tried to speak but I interrupted,

"But not always and I promise not to do it again." I said which relaxed her and chilled her out from all her worries.

"I love you Prince. I love you so much!!!!!!!" she declared extending all her words loudly and as a small baby without even caring for the presence of her elder sister.

I still remember the moment when she had spoken those magical words as if casting a magical spell on me. She was so happy that she did not even realize that it was our last evening together in Kashmir, the beautiful land of my first love. Or maybe she did not want me to realize the fact and get to a depressing mood. It was already 3.00 in the morning. A declaration came from the middle of the room.

"Guys, I think we should go to bed and take some rest to avoid any kind of exertion tomorrow. We have to take our train from Jammu." Minti said although she did not want to break the party mood. I was upset. I did not want a partition from my sweetheart. But the only hint of happiness came when I found out that the Rajasthani family was boarding the same train as our consort the next day.

* * * *

Chapter - 8

4th of April, 2009

"Good morning baby", Salu said taking me into a surprise, she kissed me on my fore head as she was trying to wake me up. But the only thing I did was, removed my pillow from under my head and kept resting on her lap. She was ready for the travel with her fragrant perfume filling the room with aroma. My roommates were also ready to take the taxi to Jammu. But Salu was still moving her hand over my head resting on her lap. This moment took me to the clouds.

"Salini, you move out from there or else the donkey is going to sleep more", Neel prompted

"Just shut up Neel", I shouted at her just to enjoy a few more moments on my baby's lap

"Get up Prince. Please baby", Salu requested as it sounded very delightful to my eardrums.

"It's already 7.30 dear", she continued as I got up with a lot of reluctance

We were chatting in our room and simultaneously getting ready to get to the breakfast table. I was still sleepy due to last night's late night party, and then followed by sleeplessness with the thoughts of one hour private chat with Salu, with the special permission from Minti.

"Ohh God I am having a severe hang over", Mayank said

"I had asked you to take Rum instead of Whisky", Rohan prompted as he always had enough and detailed knowledge about alcohol. He believed in sharing free wisdom about alcohol with each and every person, without knowing whether it was required or not. His habit of free distribution sometimes racked and ruined my nervous system.

"Do you need a drink more darling", Neel spoke sarcastically as her usual habit of extending things.

"That's the demerit of not having a girlfriend", I said emphasizing on my last four words stretching the word "not" and reminding Mayank about his statement given last night. I didn't know whether he remembered the last night happenings. He was very heavily drunk when he had spoken those words. Salini looked at me and gave a monumental smile. Wow that was more than sufficient for me.

"Every dog has a day, dude", Mayank replied back still making stupid noises out of pain. May be he had summoned up the last night phenomenon.

"Yes, my friend..." I tried to continue the argument but I was restricted by Sweety

"Now stop your cat fighting idiots and rush to the breakfast table, Mr. and Mrs. Chittra have been waiting for us since long." Sweety ordered as old grandmothers do to their grandchildren.

And we followed her instructions as submissive kids and swiftly towards the restaurant. But it was becoming hard pressed situation for me to gulp down my breakfast. I could even visualize the same problem with Salu. There was absolute wreckage in my digestive system. But Mr. Chittra was enjoying his idli and sambar. The Idli sick dumbo did not have any reaction about the last breakfast on the table of Hotel Green Valley. I really didn't have any idea of why he preferred south Indian breakfast even though he was in the northern most part of India. My final conclusion was, maybe he was bored of what was served at home for years and wanted a change over when he was away. He was consuming those idlis as if they were the last ones in his life, and then Mrs. Chittra would put him away from his favourite idlis. He could have eaten the breakfast made for all the south Indian people all alone in southern part of India.

We finally parcelled ourselves into the tata sumo saying good bye to the beautiful place. I paid a heavy tip to the manager for allotting us a room near the junior Chittra's and making my love life successful. Mayank, Minti, Salu and I occupied the last seat and the rest managed with the available places. Rohan had to share the front seat with Mr. Chittra. Every fifteen minutes he would look back with innocent eyes which demanded rescue. He would also make faces looking at me as if Mr. Chittra was manhandling him or may be sexually assaulting him. I felt sorry for not helping him out. But till I was spending my time with Salu it was difficult to divert my attention. I knew Mr. Chittra was not going to rape him in a moving car so I didn't care about what was the reason after his off-the-wall reactions.

I was resting on my sweetheart's shoulder with my hand entangled with hers. I knew if one of the senior Chittra's would look back we would be in great danger but I never cared for. I loved her and was ready to face anything for her. When I thought about my act, it seemed stupid. But I was in love. People tend to perform all the stupid acts when they are in love. To our good luck no one turned for supervision. But Minti was regularly scaring me with her deceptive looks. She was looking at me as if I had bitten her sister's lips in front of a big crowd. I absolutely didn't care for anything, till Salu didn't have any problem. I feel stealing is not bad till you are not caught. So, I proved to be a good thief without being caught by the senior Chittra's.

We reached the Jammu station in the evening. We had to wait for the train which was three hours late from the expected time of arrival. That meant I got three more extended hours with Salu, but presence of her parents didn't allow me to have a heart full talk with her. We were making fun in the station when an idli vendor passed in front of us. The idli sick villain was looking at it as a kid staring at the chocolate stores. To my surprise he went for some of them in the station after a heavy snack before few minutes in a restaurant. He offered others for it but all refused. He could even have those idlis, if offered in front of a cremation ground.

We were waiting for our train when I saw a blind old man on the platform searching for help. But the self-absorbed crowd never wanted to misspend their time on helping the poor old man. I could also call myself one of those ego-centric people who didn't want to give a helping hand to the helpless man. Suddenly I could see Salu moving towards the man. I think she could see the need for help in the eyes of the man, who didn't even have an eye. She went right to him and had some short conversation. I could never hear them, as I was standing at a distance far from them. She held his hand and moved towards the ticket counter, bought a ticket for him and left him on the platform. I felt guilty for not having helped the old man but at the same time something else was going on in my heart. This incident made me so badly affected that I started helping helpless people whom I meet on the roads. This occurrence had raised the level of respect I had for the sweet little girl of mine.

The train had arrived and we saw our names in the chart list and both the groups had their names in two different far away compartments of the train. I wanted them to be with us but couldn't expect so many co-incidences at a time. I wasn't happy but wanted to kiss Salu at the moment. Something stopped me; my inner voice, said it would cause a serious damage to my image in front of the senior Chittra's.

* * * *

"Come on man, how many more hours are you going to spend with them", Raghav said pointing his finger in disagreement with Mayank. Mayank had planned to bring Salu and Minti with us, and exchange seats with Raghav and Rohan instead of them near the senior Chittra's. I knew it well that he was doing it for Minti and not for me. But I didn't have any problem because I was also going to take the benefit.

"Please dude, you can't do it for your own friend", Mayank said emotionally as I nodded my head in agreement.

"Come on man no emotional dramas. You know I can't handle these emotional stuff", Raghav said

I looked at Rohan for help but didn't say anything. I thought my eyes were doing the work well. Though he didn't speak I could see ignorance. The revenge for the car stuff which he had to face the whole 12 hours during the journey was clearly visible on his face. But finally my emotional eyes could not stop him agree to Mayank's offer. He stood up strong from his seat and spoke,

"Come on Raghav can't we do this much for our best friends."

This was the best thing we seven were really strong in, eye contact. We could speak to each other with our eyes. We did not require words to do them for us. Even the girls could speak with their soft eyes and capture out thoughts. We have many situations where we used this skill of ours to escape from a cop or a gangster but I think this is obviously not a place to discuss those things.

They went to the Chittra's accompanied by Aditi, Sweety and most importantly the drama queen of our group, Neel, without whom we had never succeeded in any of our plans as our past records. Aditi, the convincing lady of our group had a good hand on everyone in the past so it was preferable to send her. Mayank and I started staring at the noisy kids near our berths after they left.

"These kids will not let us sleep tonight." Mayank said

"What?" I said with a jerk as I was absent minded looking at the cute babies playing and making noise.

"I said these kids are not going to let me sleep." Mayank repeated his words again in a rough voice this time. He was actually disturbed by the sore noise made by the kids. But who the hell cared about the sleep if Salu was there with me.

"Sorry guys", Neel said as she came running faster than the Rajdhani express and bumping on to me with a shock. We (Mayank and I) jumped up from our seats probably with our hearts in our mouth. Her entry was like a train running inside another train.

"What!!!! Fuck man!!!! And what was the sorry for?" Mayank shouted with a terrified voice standing up on his seat.

"What happened? And I feel that was a nice entry" Neel said as if ignorant of our shock at her sudden horrified entry. Even the noisy kids started crying louder, creating a higher intensity of noise. They also had been terrified at her entry.

"Do you want to murder us giving us a heart attack?" Mayank spoke before I could recover from the shock of her unexpected entry.

"But I always do it, no", She said with a childish voice. Girls know it well how to melt boys whatever situation they might be in. She always had the habit of apologizing without telling sorry.

"Shut the bull shit right now and tell me what happened? Where are Salu and Minti? And where are the others?" I asked

"I am sorry they did not agree to come with us", the drama queen spoke with her stupid wry smile. I never liked it whenever she smiled that way. It always meant something fishy was going on around.

"What!!!!!! Who didn't agree? I know it must be the idli sick bastard." I said as my voice went louder this time.

"No, Salu said she didn't want to come", She spoke again with a damn wry smile. Her smiles were now getting on to my nerves.

"What the fuck man!!!!! She can't do this." I spoke as I could see a girl with an elegant black salwar kameez coming towards our berth even before my sentence was complete. It was Salu and Minti coming along with Sweety and Aditi. They were almost fifty meters away. I thanked God that they were not nearby when I called their dad an idli sick bastard. Raghav and Rohan had to manage the whole night with my hopeful in-laws. I was sure at least Rohan was not going to be manhandled in the train.

"Wow...They are here", I said and sprang on to Mayank to hug him.

"Idiot, you were playing a prank on us." Mayank spoke to Neel with a bit of flirty smile which he always had talking to girls.

They soon arrived and we had an extensive conversation together with Salu as usual comfortably lying on my arms. I knew it was burning the young youth passengers next to us like the hot chicken wings of the KFC. But I enjoyed burning people out of jealousy with hot cheeks entangled with me. And now that I had my love with me it was more fun doing it.

"Let's sleep now", Minti said with a tired voice. I really didn't understand whether she was so much addicted to her sleeping habit or she loved fucking up my romantic moments with her sister.

"We can't sleep with those kids roaring all the night!!!!" Aditi exclaimed elongating the chat process. I wanted to tell her I love you, but avoided due to Minti's presence.

We finally had to act according to her stupid command of sleeping. That was so stupid of a killer to obey his girlfriend's sister's command and go to sleep, when his girlfriend wanted to have a longer chat with him. I suggested Salu to take the middle berth of the left side as I was taking the upper one. So that we could chat a little more before we could actually catch sleep. I was making the best use of the time we were provided with. But my suggestion had struck the ears of Minti and she gave me a scaring look. And her eyes trying to speak to me *"Don't try to do anything wrong with my sister."* My eyes replied back to her *"Come on you idiot, we are in the train and I can't have sex with your sister, so just stop looking at me like a buffoon."* My looks were stern enough for her to understand what was going on in my mind.

The girls started opening their vanities to have a final touch up before sleep. I obviously don't understand the logic of having a makeup just before you go to bed. One could never understand girls until and unless they want you to know them. I could see Salu removing her chocolate coloured lipstick and applying lip gloss instead of that. The colour of her lipstick had increased my appetite of having a chocolate or maybe it was just an urge to kiss her. But the audiences around us were the great criminals to stop me kiss her chocolate coloured lipstick.

I managed to speak to Salu for more than an hour leaning my head down to her and my hands completely in her control. I was sure to have a neck pain the next morning but I didn't care. The attraction of her being with me never stopped me facing any difficulties.

"Get up dumbos we are going to reach Delhi in next two hours", a fully recognized voice came up to my berth as I bent down to see, it was none other than the drama queen who never cared about the place she was creating a drama, Neel. She was trying to sprinkle water on all the guys with a plastic glass. She could not use a jug as she used in the hotel to wake all of us, due to unavailability of the jug.

I decided to move down before the idiotic works of Neel reach out of my patience. I went down and straight away slept resting my head on Salu's lap. I felt it was the best place to sleep peacefully after my mom's lap. But the stupid idiotic creatures never allowed me to sleep. May be they were jealous of what I received from my sweetheart. She moved her hands over my head which badly tempted me to sleep more.

"Get up idiot, uncle may be coming for a round", Aditi said and I had to obey her instructions. I never knew why she was so apprehensive about all these fatuous stuffs. To some extent I even didn't want to take a risk on anything which would take me away from my girlfriend.

The New Delhi station had arrived and now was the time to part from my sweatheart. Though I was too overexcited to meet my family but I was dejected to get away from my girlfriend. We said good bye to each other exchanging our cell phone numbers. It was out of the reach of my killer brain that this was the last moment I was going to see my Salu. I never knew when I was going to see her the next time. I could see pain in her eyes but I was forced to stay back not hugging her. Later I was guilty but it was the right decision. Very soon the Rajasthan group had moved out of our sight. We had to wait for our train to Odisha.

* * * *

Chapter - 9

The train had arrived and we took our seats. I was still in a bad mood and missing Salu badly this time. I switched on my cell phone which was switched off for the last five days since we had stepped into Jammu. This was due to the internal security reasons of Jammu and Kashmir which avoided the networks of cell phones of other states other than their own state. I was expecting my mom's call as I was missing her too. I hadn't had a word with my mom and dad since I had left Delhi last. I was sitting on the place near the window and was troubled by the mixed feelings of missing Salu and the joy of reaching home.

Suddenly my cell phone vibrated with ring tone of airtel which the most wanted tone of the time. The screen showed an unknown number. It wasn't a call from Odisha, the number was from somewhere outside the state. I picked up the call with a bit of hesitation.

"Hello", I said

"Hello….what's my naughty boy doing?" a sweet voice came from the other side. It was Salu. She was calling me from the washroom of the train. I could then feel the exact extent I missed her. My eyes were numbed. I could not believe that she had called me so early. Though we could not have a long conversation, due to the disturbance made by the noise of the train, but it had relaxed me a lot. Finally she kept the phone down saying "I Love you my sweet naughty baby." Her sweet words could kill me someday with happiness.

I could see a young guy with a book related to sex. Those books should not have been opened in public at least when girls are around you. Not at least in India!! So we decided to deter him. I looked at Neel giving her a signal that it was time for some serious mischief. We didn't do any such mischief since long due to the presence of the Chittra's. She could easily understand my point and nodded her pretty head in agreement. It was fun time. She was very good at creating a drama anywhere and everywhere. She moved out of the compartment to another waiting for our signal to enter. As soon as the guy entered into the last few pages of his books Raghav missed a call for her to act. She immediately jumped on the man without allowing him to think much.

"Hey baby, why do you read such books when such a hot girl is present near you", Neel spoke to the guy with a very seductive voice. I could bet a hundred dollars on her now that she could seduce any handsome boy with her voice. On the other hand we were ready for her rescue if something grim happens, as you never know a boy's mood. But to our good luck the guy just moved out of the place hiding his face. And we laughed for next twenty minutes including an aunty sharing a berth in our compartment.

Indubitably Salu's call had eased up my worries and I was able to have my dinner peacefully. We had terrible fun in our bogie creating nuisance with other passengers. Raghav and Rohan had opened up their original color which was hidden for the last few days. I never knew whether they were doing it to show respect to Salu and Minti or something. But we had unquestionably missed our fun time. It was difficult to control us then. I am sure some passengers must have cursed us for our idiotic works.

* * * *

Finally we landed on the capital of Odisha, Bhubaneswar. It was undoubtedly a pleasurable moment for me to meet my parents. I went out of the railway station to see my mom and dad standing with a lot of excitement to see me. It was a moment of joy for me. I had spent a full week away from my home all alone. And that too for the first time in the whole life since I was out of the labour ward of the hospital. I went running to my mom and hugged her after touching her feet. I could see her eyes wet. But I felt it would be good to keep my mouth shut at that moment. Sometimes keeping your mouth shut is the best thing you can ever do. We bid good bye to all the members of the group and decided to meet in our usual place in the evening.

Our usual place was a destined stone, big enough to let seven of us a place to lie down under a tree. The spot was discovered by all of us about a year ago. We had big fights with our opponent gang on the same spot and many other mischievous activities undergone. The place was situated in an interior with only few houses around it and rest belonging to the forest.

I reached home with my parents and decided to freshen up and have some nutriment before I would starve. I waited for Salu's call for long after some delicious homemade cuisine. She didn't call. Last night was her last call and I was dying to listen to her sweet voice. I was trying to apply the killer rule of wait till the girl calls you but everything went in vain. I waited for two hours and then finally couldn't resist dialling her number. The killer was no more a killer; he was dead, as he had fallen in love. I don't think any of my killer rules would work anymore. She picked up my call within just one ring. May be she was waiting for my call.

"Hello, my naughty boy", she said in a very mellifluous voice. Her voice had always made me feel so good and relaxed. Each time I heard it tend to be sweeter than the last time I had heard it. It was more harmonious than the sugared almonds.

"Have you forgotten me?" I asked

"How can I forget my sweet honey baby", she said lengthening the third last word of her statement. I never counted the names she had given me. But I always thought a dictionary could be easily written out of those.

"Why didn't you call me then?" I said as I was still acting to be strong with my words

"I am so sorry my sweet Prince, I was just waiting for your call", she said twisting her words and this time it was so endearing that I could not stop myself kissing her. We had a long conversation for about an hour, it didn't matter to me much even if it was an STD call. Though I knew STD calls were now going to hit me hard on my back financially after the month ends.

It was time for me to reach our spot to meet my gang. The word gang usually meant bad but it sounds trendy when hot blood flows in your body. As soon as I reached,

"So the lover boy is here", Neel said as the idiot had to speak every time but I loved being teased with Salu. The whole group had been waiting for me for an hour. I had delayed my arrival due to Salu's call. I never dared to look at the watch when she was on call or maybe I never wanted to.

"Ya, I am here", I said with a shy smile which was never out of the killer before.

"What next now?" Raghav asked looking at me.

"What do you mean?" I said as I could not understand a single word which he spoke.

"I meant who is the next targeted girl?" he asked.

"Hey she is my girlfriend and not a target, and she is the one I love", I said.

"What!!!!!!!!!!!" Aditi was shocked.

"So you decided to be with the Rajasthani for the rest of the life?" Raghav asked.

"Yes and stop calling her Rajasthani she has a good name SALINI", I answered strongly elongating Salu's name which I had never done ever before. Raghav gave me wry smiles as if I had just cracked a joke. But his attitude could not be ignored as I never liked to stay with the same girl for more than a month. I knew it well that I had seriously dumped myself into something called love but now I didn't care for anything other than Salu.

* * * *

Chapter - 10

A long time had passed by after our return from the Kashmir trip. We had been enjoying almost every day after our exams. But now was the real testing time, the result time. Everybody had a thrill in their heart. The toppers had an expectation of topping the state or the country, the average students folding their hands before the lord to have a decently good score and the below average students prayed to God to get a passing score. Everyone bribed the lord in their own way.

I could find no such bribing or worries in any of our group member's face. I was the only one who was most worried about the results. It was the day of our results and we were sitting under the tree and watching a comic bollywood movie-Hera Pheri on Mayank's laptop. It was shame on us to watch movies at such times. But Baba Mayank Dev had different views about the fact. Before we started watching the movie, he said,

"My dear disciples, when you watch comic movies before exams or results you will be easily controlling your feelings and emotions. Worries will not touch your heart or soul. You will feel the immense pleasure of life." He spoke and I am sure Baba Ramdev would have got complexes by his statements and the way he spoke them.

"Jai Ho Baba Mayank dev ki." Neel said and the statement was repeated by all of us. Mayank gave a hand signal of accepting the appreciations.

"What do you have to tell about porn movies Baba" Sweety asked trying to pull his leg. But he was smart enough to answer the queries.

"My dear disciples, they are the utmost peace giving videos created by some of the pure hearted people to give human beings immense pleasure and satisfaction when they don't have a source" he said with a very grave and serious tone as if he was delivering a devotional lecture on the astha channel.

"Some more extensive knowledge on the topic Baba" Rohan asked.

"My dear disciple, too much knowledge on the topic is going to cause damage to your brain. You should take knowledge by instalments" he said and sat down to switch on his laptop.

The movie was over and we still had an hour before the declaration of the results. The movie had actually relaxed everyone with a hearty laugh. Perhaps Baba Mayank Dev had pronounced the correct statements. But I could see a bit of stress on everyone's face now. No one wanted to display their tension. We wanted to keep cool before anything happened. Our group was the best one. We didn't want to express our stress and stress out others.

The time finally came. We could view the peon moving out of the staff room. He was proceeding towards the notice board. Our heart was beating fast. As he came close to the notice board all of us stood in a line with hand in hand with prayers on our lips. Then we made a circle as the Indian cricket team does before the start of the innings. But it was actually the end of innings for us. We were going to move out of the college after the results.

"All the best guys don't worry" I said but I was the guy who was most tensed.

"All the best, let's go now" Mayank said as we dispersed towards the notice board. I could hear the peon mumbling that twenty one students had failed the exam. I prayed to god to keep all of us away from those twenty one. I was praying more for my friends than me. As soon as I came close to the notice board I started searching for our names. I could trace out everyone's name in the list except mine. My heart beats stopped. I started breathing faster. *Have I failed to secure passing marks in the exams?* I thought. My eyes had started becoming red. I was wet with the sweat of nervousness.

"Hey Gyan your name is in the other list" Sahil, a thin and lean boy shouted, a classmate of mine. His starving looks suggested as if he had not seen food for years. I started searching in other list. The list displayed that I had scored 77.5%!! I felt stupid of myself for searching my name in the 60 to 75% list. I had never expected such a score. But it was God's grace. I was successful in scoring the marks. Mayank and Raghav ran close to me picking me up in the air. I was in fact the top scorer of my group. I was more than happy about this. All our group members had passed the test with more than 60%. It was unimaginable but true. We had never touched our books before the last day of the examination.

"We should have a party tonight" Neel suggested

"Yes we should have a grand party tonight" I said and everyone looked at me with their shot up eyes, as I usually avoided parties. But today we deserved it.

I called up Salu and told her about the results. She was in the temple bribing god for our results. She had not taken a sip of water till I called her. She told me if she prayed to God without taking food god gets impressed. I didn't believe in any such theories. The thing which impressed me was that she had been fasting since the morning for all of us not only for me.

"Ready for the party" Neel said as she stepped out of the house. She was the last one to arrive. Everyone starred at her with an angry look, but none of us spoke. We were waiting for her in front of her room since thirty minutes but she was busy dressing up.

"What?" she asked looking at herself from top to bottom to check if her dress was perfect? I don't know why girls always take the look so seriously. She looked at the rear view mirror of the car, to check out her face. She didn't notice our frustration and went inside the car. May be she didn't want to notice our frustration and pack up a good amount of scolding.

We went to the same disco where we had been before our exams. My eyes could trace out the girl who had slapped Mayank. She was on a table sitting alone. May be she was waiting for someone. But I could see a trace of perturbation on her face. I told Mayank to apologize to her for what he had done that day, even though he didn't have any idea of what he had actually done. He was reluctant in going near her. I asked Aditi to go near her and ask her to join us. She had already exhibited her convincing skills in some of the impossible situations before the trip to Kashmir.

I could see Aditi talk to her for long and at last the girl got up from her seat and walked towards us accompanied by Aditi. Mayank was freezing even though the temperature in the disco was not as cool as that in Kashmir. Mayank held my hand tight under the table. His hands seemed cooler than my glass of soft drink. May be he was reminded about the slap.

"Guys this is Reshma" Aditi introduced her to all of us.

"Hello Reshma" all of us said in unison except Mayank.

"Hello every one and Hello to the young man, who was slapped by me few days back, because of exhibiting his efficiency in kissing girls" she said in a very jolly voice. She still remembered Mayank. Mayank put his neck down for a second in shame. May be he realized what he had done for the well deserved slap. Reshma looked an absolute sex bomb with her tiny, micro mini skirt and her black top which had almost squeezed her bosoms. Her black top was short enough for her naval ring to be visible.

"You idiot, you tried to kiss her that night" Neel shouted at Mayank but I think he never even cared to give his ear to her statement.

"Listen, I don't know what I had done with you that day but I am very sorry for what I had done. I was badly drunk that night. So please forgive..." Mayank spoke without breathing in and he was injected by Reshma. He was speaking at a speed more than the speed of the lightening.

"Hey relax dear. I understand but you need to be punished for the behaviour" She said looking at Mayank

"What punishment do you want to give me? You had already punished me that day with your sweet slap." Mayank asked sarcastically as if in a bombshell. He still remembered the tight slap he had received from the soft hands of Reshma.

"My boy friend has ditched me today. He is there on the dance floor with another girl. Go and slap him" she said as she pointed at a dark looking guy dancing with a girl on the dance floor. I could never believe that such a bad looking guy could be Reshma's boy friend who looked so pretty and undoubtedly hot.

"Is that the only punishment?" Mayank asked for a confirmation with a deliberate pause after her statement. And now Reshma looked jerked. She didn't know that Mayank was brave enough to hit anyone at anytime.

"What do you mean?" she asked with a source of agitation

"Nothing I am going to do it but I have a condition" Mayank said with a deceiving smile. This guy could never get away from his flirty statements.

"What is your condition dear?" she enquired reluctantly as if she felt Mayank could never slap her ex-boy friend.

"You have to spend the evening with our group" Mayank said

"Yes done, I would love to." she said confidently. Mayank pushed his chair back. He walked towards the dance floor. Raghav walked behind him to check that he didn't create much of a mess. All our eyes were stuck to the dance floor. Everyone was waiting for Mayank's action. Mayank went straight to the guy pointed by Reshma. Mayank re-confirmed that he was the same person, looking back at Reshma. After getting a confirmation from Reshma with her thumbs up, he pulled the guy from his shoulder. And then went the bang on the face. Reshma had asked Mayank to slap him but he had banged the guy down with one punch. The guy got up with all his efforts and tried to attack. But the rest of the work was done by

Raghav. Raghav smashed the guy with all his force. And flat on the ground fell the body. I could see blood on Raghav's hand. He had broken the guy's nose. The guy was bleeding badly in his nose. The poor guy didn't have any idea about the thrashing. The bouncer's arrival at the spot didn't have any effect on anyone. They were just the audience to the scene. Mayank walked back to his seat with Raghav. I could see a different glaze on Reshma's face. She offered to dance with Mayank. Mayank agreed without any hesitation.

It was the first time when Mayank didn't touch his drink and preferred to spend all the time with a girl. Mayank without his drink in a disco was an absolute shock for all of us. I had restrictions so I had no chance to have a drink. Now we had two people in complete senses who could drive us back i.e. Mayank and me. I took the driving seat and asked Mayank to be comfortable on the seat beside me. After dropping everyone in their respective places I drove to Mayank's place to drop him. On our arrival at his place,

"Don't you think Reshma is nice?" he asked. I didn't want to tell anything so I gave a colossal smile giving him a confirmation.

"Thanks dude" he said as my smile was enough for him to understand my reactions. He moved away and I drove back home.

* * * *

Chapter - 11

My cell phone rang with the ringtone of "kaise tum mujhe mil gayi" from the movie Gajni. The movie had become a craze for the entire youngster, especially for the well built body and hair style of Aamir Khan. The vibration of the phone woke me up. I could see the screen flashing "Salu calling". I received her call struggling to open my eyes and trying to pull out myself from the heavy blanket over me.

"Good morning my naughty boy", Salu said

"Good morning baby", I said still struggling to pull myself out of the peaceful long sleep.

"So what's my naughty baby doing, doesn't seem that he is out of his bed", she said and I never understood why she used the adjective naughty for me though I hadn't done anything naughty with her. But I loved it when she used the same word for me. We had a long chat before I could get ready for college. I never wanted to keep the phone down but I didn't either want to miss the first day of my college.

I dressed up with my uniform and moved out to find Mayank with his black Scorpio, the most wanted vehicle of our group. It was the only one that was available anytime you wanted it. Wow was only the expression I could exclaim at the situation as I was getting late. He had been there as an angel to help me out. I could breathe a shy of relief now. I entered the car and spoke

"Thanks dude"

"I knew you are going to be late. I found your phone to be continuously busy this morning, so I rushed to give you a lift till your bus stand", Mayank said

I didn't have any answer for his statement as a spontaneous smile came to my face. It wasn't a fake one but a true one like our friendship. I just prayed god that our friendship never broke. I kept quiet and listened to all the scolding for being late and careless, which included a slang in every two or maximum three words. More than scolding I could call it the way of interaction of our group.

We reached the bus stop. Mayank managed to stop the bus. It was an inch difference between the bus and the car. If the bus driver would have delayed a second applying the brakes then we would have been thrashed along with the car. My first day of college would have been the last day. I was left dumb when I stepped out of the car. I could not speak anything. There would be no effect on Mayank even if I had spoken something; it was the usual way he drove his car. I was saved from facing a severe accident by a fraction of seconds.

When I entered the bus, I could see the old dirty looking driver mumbling to himself. May be he was abusing Mayank but I didn't care. The best part was that I didn't miss the first day of my new college. I went straight to the window seat saying bye to Mayank as the bus moved.

* * * *

Chapter - 12

"Shut up you bloody criminal", Mayank was shouting at a tall, black, fat and angry man who was bleeding by his left hand. We were having a momentous street fight with few strangers for passing comments on Neel.

Mayank looked at me and asked

"Do you need a doc?" as I was surprised at his change of statements

"I think I will need some medical help soon", I spoke as my right hand was full of blood due to a deep cut during the initial fights. The air was still hot; I had smashed down one of the opponents on the bonnet of the black car belonging to Mayank, the car which had helped me to attend my first college class. I repented but the time I did the damage I was out of my sense. And Mayank had the worst reaction I had ever seen. He reacted as if he was waiting to use the common toilet in Taj Mahal for more than an hour in a queue. The bonnet was bumped in about five inches towards the ground. In return one of our foes had stabbed my right hand with a sharp blade.

The brawl continued as the rotund rivals fell on the ground not tolerating the blows from Raghav, Rohan, Mayank and me. The karate chops from Neel, Aditi and Sweety were also a great help to us in sustaining the fight. The audiences were amazed to see three sex bombs indulged in the fight. They enjoyed watching the girls more than the fight. I could see some middle aged men with their mouth wide open which could allow a swarm of honey bees into them. Sweety, Aditi and Neel were the black belt karate champions, rest of us just being the street fight champions.

The arrival of the police van stopped the far reaching fight. Someone from the crowd had called the police to take the control of the fight. May be he wanted to be rewarded with a trophy for his brave work of inviting the cops. My heart beats had almost stopped on seeing the cops. I had never before seen so many cops from such a close yonder. They looked like humans in fact they were human beings but their uniform caused a threat in my mind. One of the junior officials looked liked Gabbar Singh from the renounced bollywood movie-Sholay, with his long combed moustache. My heart was almost shifted in my mouth but Mayank was still continuing to scold the foes with his usual slangs. I could not understand why he was doing that. But I could see his gestures with his eyes towards Raghav even though I could not understand anything. Everything was going over my head as Bret Lee's bouncers.

Raghav took the senior official to the corner of the black Scorpio and handed him an amount of five hundred bucks. Then I came to know about the fishy plans of Mayank. The pleased and bribed inspector soon became our slave and ordered the reappeared Gabbar Singh to arrest the three drunken fatsos. After all in India money always has an upper hand. Even hundreds of Anna Hazare's may not be sufficient to eradicate the corrupt minds of this beautiful nation. And Raghav was the best person with us who dealt with the cops in a deviating way.

"Let's run to the doc, he is bleeding a lot", Neel said with her voice tensed and terrified looks which made me more horrified.

"It's okay now I will manage", I said with confidence filled in my voice. I never knew where the confidence had come from. May be due to the last few blows I had banged on the face of the man who had stabbed my hand in the later half of the fight.

"Shut up dumbo, let's see the doctor now", Sweety ordered as she always had the habit of ordering without taking anyone's consent. But this habit of hers sometimes made all of us feel in a safe and matured hand.

Neel had covered my wound with her pink handkerchief. I could feel the fragrance of her perfume from the hanky, even though it was completely absorbed by my blood. I had almost lost more than half a bottle blood by the time we reached the hospital. My hands were wet with sweat and my vision wasn't clear enough. I felt as if someone had carefully placed fishing net between my eye lid and eye lens. I needed assistance to stand erect. I took the support of Mayank's shoulder. The sweat from my hand was flowing down towards the wound. The mixture of the sweat, blood and the cut had started to inflate the burning sensation of my hand. The doctor arrived and did his job. I started staring at the known faces to avoid looking at the scissors and injections. I started feeling ok. I was provided a glass of glucose water by a fairly hot looking nurse that made me feel more than ok. I was now fit enough to play a T-20 cricket match but unfortunately we didn't have a team big enough to do that. And most importantly if I would have shared my idea of playing cricket my head would have been thrashed into pieces by my group members.

I was dropped home by Raghav with his stylish Pulsar bike which was a newly launched version. We were all crazy about his bike and sometimes he would also lend us his bike to have a short ride. He took care of his bike as a newly born baby. But most importantly I was at home now and I had to think of an excuse for my cut to mom and dad. As soon as I stepped into the house I got the same reactions from my mom as I had expected before. She got a shock and then gave me a hug to make me feel at home. It was a typical Indian mother style of welcoming an injured son to the home. I narrated an imaginary accident, where I was thrashed down by an over speeding bike. I had to cook up a fig mental story to my parents with detailed explanation about how the bike hit me, what angle the bike was coming from and how I got such a big cut on my hand. I was over loaded with various questions about my illusory tale. Each time I was fired a question, bang went the answer like the space rocket with full confidence. But each time I spoke, a sword of guilt stabbed me on my back. Yes, I was guilty of telling lies to my parents but I had no other way out. I could not expect applauses from them, if I had told them that their only son had just won a street fight with some goons. And escaped being arrested due to Raghav's quick-witted bribing the cops. I soon released myself from the crime branch type interrogation of my parents and freshened up to feel better.

On having my dinner I went to my room comfortably placing my tired and wounded body on the cozy bed. And resting my back on the soft pillow, I took out my cell phone from my pocket to find out whether someone had tried to reach me and I had missed it. When I took out the phone and unlocked the keypad, each and every word of expression was on the tip of my tongue.

GOD!!! DAMN!!!! OH FUCK MAN!!!!! Yes, someone had tried to reach me and had tried 157 times!!!! I had 157 missed calls and 33 text messages from Salu! How could I miss her call? I started blaming myself as my eyes carefully ran down her messages. Every message had a crying smiley at the end. I still remember a message which had touched me a lot *"Prince I am sorry if I have hurt you somewhere, please forgive me and receive my call."* This one had a lot of crying smiley which made my eyes almost wet. Some of the messages only had crying smiley without any text written on it. But I could not find any messages which expressed anger. It was very shocking not to find any messages which expressed anger, but it was true. I had hurt her badly. A mixed feeling of guilt and anger had squeezed me. Should I call her now? Will she be angry with me? Will she receive my call? Many such questions were oscillating over my head. I gathered all my courage as if I had to visit the cage of an angry and hungry lioness and then dialed her number. I was holding the phone with my right hand and with my left hand I had my fingers crossed. My hysterical brain was busy counting the number of rings. The call was picked up on the fifth ring.

"What do you think of yourself? Idiot", a voice came from other side. I could not believe that my Salu could be so harsh on me. It was someone else. It was a known voice of another girl. Who could it be?

"Hello ma'am, who is it?" I spoke softly with a surprise as I looked at the cell phone's screen to check that I had called Salu and no one else. The dialing screen showed Salu on call.

"What the hell do you want to prove?" the voice spoke with full of fury to which I had a hint of who the person was.

"Is it Minti?" I questioned not bothering to answer her question on what I wanted to prove.

"Yes and why did you make my sister cry the whole day?" she continued her process of shouting at me.

"What? Was she crying?" I banged the questions

"Yes the whole day she was crying in her closed room", she said and continued to give me a circumstantial description of what had happened. I was feeling guilty and wanted to talk to her immediately. I was least interested in listening to her long Vedic descriptions now. But I could not talk to my sweetheart. She was sleeping. Minti had fed her some fruits and tapped her head till she had slept, as per Minti's stretched out explanations. I kept quiet till she had finished.

"I had an accident, tell her to call me when she is awake, but don't tell her about the accident", I said and hung up without giving her a chance to speak, although she wanted to speak something. May be she was guilty of bursting all her aspiration out on me without letting me speak. But I wasn't at all worried for Minti's sorry. The thing which killed me was my blameworthiness of hurting my angel.

I could not sleep after the short chat with Minti about Salu's condition. I changed sides on my bed with an ambivalent feeling of guilt for lying to my parents and hurting my paragon, my sweetheart, my Salu. These thoughts were hovering over my head when my cell phone beeped to indicate an incoming text message. I got up from my bed to look at my bed clock. It showed 2.00 am. I checked the message, it was Salu!! She wrote

"Is my cutty pie awake?" This message included only a single crying smiley unusual from her last messages which had loads of those.

"Yes my Angel and am really sorry" I sent including a crying smiley to my text. Soon my phone beeped on arrival of her reply.

"Can we talk now, baby?" This one did not include any crying smiley. On seeing this SMS I didn't trouble myself replying instead dialled her number. She picked up my call on the first ring. May be she was expecting my call not a text reply.

"Baby", she said and started crying.

"Why is my Angel crying?" I asked although I knew that the reason of her sobbing was me. It seemed stupid on my side to ask her such an idiotic questions but it was unintentional. I wasn't ready for the situation. I had expected her to rap me over the knuckles as her sister had already done earlier in the evening but it was a situation happening in the opposite direction of my thoughts. I could not tolerate her tears. It was very difficult to stop her tear flow as it was more like a heavy water fall which did not have any intension to stop. I managed to stop her but it took a long fifteen minutes before she spoke.

"Why didn't you receive my call Prince?" she fired the question as she stopped the long process of her cry. I hadn't expected such an unexpected question coming into action so early in our conversation. Girls are much unexpected type. They always do things which are out of your thought at the point of time. I was quickly making up my mind to narrate the story of the bike accident which I had already explained my parents.

"Stop being upset, Prince", she said even though I hadn't made a hint of noise. Only drops of tears were flowing down my eyes which obviously didn't make any noise. I could not understand how she came to know about it. And for the first time my mind had to accept the fact that the stud was no more a stud. He had become a real lover boy.

"I am not upset baby", I spoke softly trying to protest her

"No lies baby, I love you no Prince", she said with so much love filled in her words that it automatically stopped my tears and she could even know that my tears had stopped.

"That's like a good boy, no, in fact that's like my naughty boy." She said emphasizing her last three words. But I could never understand how could she know what was happening on the other side of the phone staying thousands of kilometers away from me, in another state.

But my task was yet not over I owed her an explanation about why I hadn't received her call. I had to explain the story of the accident but when my mouth opened it started to narrate the perfect street fight we had during the whole day, the cops and their reactions, my reaction during the arrival of the cops, our rotund and drunken foes and all other stuffs. I proudly spoke about my blows which dumped the black car's bonnet towards the ground. I do not know why I did that. But something from inside me told me not to lie to her. May be it was my soul which had fallen in love with her.

I had to take a long lecture from my Miss Salini Chittra after my explanation but I loved it. I wanted her to proceed further as I hadn't listened to her voice for the whole day. It is always lovely to be scolded by your beloved when you want them to speak and you just want to be a silent listener. After she had completed

"Your voice is really sweet, angel, especially when you deliver a lecture a lecture!!", I said

"What!!!!" she was shocked as if I had used some of Mayank's favourite slangs in front of the Queen Victoria.

"What?" I asked with more of an intension to tease her than asking a question. I pretended as if I dint know what I had just spoken.

"You think I was just delivering a lecture and you concentrated on my voice quality!!!" She said

"I did not mean that but your voice seemed cute when you were at a pace", I said teasing her

"Okay so Mr. Gyan do you do the same in your classes?" She asked with her voice growing romantic.

"Not exactly as we do not have any female teacher whose voice is as sweet as my Angel", I said

"Is it Prince?" She spoke stretching the words longer with her voice turning more romantic and flirty

"Yes but I used to do it in my tenth grade with our environment science teacher, she had a really sweet voice…" I continued but was halted by her

"What do you mean? Was it only voice that seemed sweet to you?" she questioned as I could feel a hint of jealousy.

"No she was actually very hot and spicy. I mean the perfect figure", I spoke trying to take a benefit out of her jealous statement

"Shut up Prince", she said confirming me her resentment.

"Why?" I questioned trying to poke fun at her.

"Just like that, please shut up", she said with her voice drowning

"Is something burning out of jealousy in Rajasthan", I said putting highly flammable petrol on the fire.

"Yes your sweet heart is burning out of jealousy no", she said finally confronting with an angry voice, which was sweeter than her smile as I had a hearty laugh first time in the day. I loved the way she used the word no at the end of her statements. It added honey to her words. It was like a sweet dish after a full course well cooked meal to me.

"I love you, my baby" I said continuing my laugh

"I hate you, go and talk to your environment science teacher", she said making an effort to show me that she was angry. But it had a different kind of sweetness in it which cannot be explained in mere word. Her efforts were gone in vain as I could not stop laughing.

"I love you Angel", I continued as the three magical words came for the first time of the day from the other side

"I love you too", she said as I felt as if I had all the happiness in the world with me now.

We continued our gabbling till it was 6.00 in the morning. I decided to directly get ready to avoid missing my college bus and my beauty queen went to bed as she had no intension of attending college after a hectic day full of weeping for me.

* * * *

Chapter - 13

"Get up Gyan, its morning", a voice hit my ear drums as I struggled to open my eyes to see who it was.

"Morning…Good morning sir…" I fumbled as I found our physics lecturer Mr. Vikram near my seat with a vexed expression. I had never noticed when he had entered the class and started teaching. I was busy in taking my day's nap.

SLAP!! SLAP!! SLAP!! Three well organized slaps on my right cheek without any further conversation as my brown skin turned red within no time. I thought *if he would have used both my cheeks then the pain would have been divided.* But it was not advisable to open my mouth as I didn't have any explanation for sleeping during the class hours. I could obviously not tell him about my previous night's late night talk with Salu.

"Get out of my class, ***sleeping beauty***" Mr. Vikram said speaking out the last two words with a louder intensity and the whole class of sixty students burst out laughing as if someone had tickled their funny bone. I felt embarrassed. I had no other option other than obeying his commands as a sincere student.

"Sir…" I tried to give an explanation cooking up something as soon as possible in my brain but it was interrupted.

"Get lost from my class; I don't need ***sleeping donkeys*** in my class room" Mr. Vikram spoke as I moved out of the class as soon as possible avoiding any other special adjectives, with my face parallel to the ground. As I was moving out of the class thoughts of smashing the face of my physics teacher came to my brain as I had done during our street fight. I wanted to place some well organized blows on his face. But it was difficult to do that in a secured college campus. And the fear of the cops was also within me especially when Raghav was not there to deal with the cops.

It was unquestionable shameful as I had to stand outside the class room. It became odd when girls passing by giggled before they started a conversation among themselves about me. The title given by my physics teacher was still revolving over my head, ***SLEEPING DONKEY*** and a ***SLEEPING BEAUTY!!!!!*** The teachers passing by just smiled and used the phrase naughty boy. I wanted to stop them and tell them "naughty boy" can only be used by my sweet heart and not by anyone else. Unfortunately I could not speak those words as I didn't face any more difficulties after being thrown out of the class with some of the special names.

I rested my body and head on the wall with my eyes closed to make people think that I was tensed for being thrown out of the class. I had actually been planning to take a short standing nap. That sounds ridiculous but I could have a peaceful uninterrupted fifteen minutes nap, before I was distracted by the period ending bell. I found Mr. Vikram coming out of the class with his usual upset looking face. He looked as if someone had pick pocketed him before few minutes.

"You can move in, Mr. SLEEPING BEAUTY", He said again emphasizing his last two words for the second time of the day.

"Thank you sir", I said with a spontaneous smile coming to my face

"Thank you for what?" he questioned with a hint of surprise.

"Nothing Sir", I said with my smile becoming more natural. I banged open the door of the class room to make my way clear to the place which was abandoned for me before fifteen minutes. He was still in confusion for what I had thanked for. I actually was thanking him for the uninterrupted fifteen minutes peaceful nap. He had an unusual facial expression as if a cricket ball had hit his private part. But I didn't care to change his expression; I wanted to actually hit a cricket ball on his private part.

I could hear the girls talk about the sleeping beauty as I was passing through the rows to my seat. It was a lunch break and I took out the phone from my pocket and dialed Mayank's number.

"Hello bro", Mayank said

"Dump the hello and come to the college gate at 12.30", I said with a frustrating voice

"Hey, what has happened to you? Is there any problem?" He enquired. I don't understand why people always have to know your problems immediately. Why can't they do whatever they are told to do at times?

"No nothing I just don't want to take the bus today." I said as I wanted to avoid any further embarrassments in the bus.

"Okay I will be there", he said and hung up.

I thought I would call Salu but then I thought I would disturb her sweet sleep. And I carried on with my second thought and started searching for my lunch box. Mom had prepared noodles and packed them in my lunch box. It had been as cold as ice cream and had taken the oval shape of my lunch box. It looked like a large artificially painted egg by a second grade student. It seemed affected by bird flu. I loved noodles when they are hot but not in the condition it was with me. I would hate it more than my greatest enemy. I could not resist calling Salu as I had nothing to do.

"Hello my sweet Prince", she said with a sleepy voice and I realized that I had disturbed her hibernation.

"What are you doing?" I asked as a stupid. I never knew how to start a conversation when I am in my rough mood.

"Was just sleeping on your lap when your call disturbed me", she said with a naughty voice. But neither I was in a mood nor a proper place getting naughty. I don't understand why girls get on to such a mood when they are out of the bed or else when they are prepared to take the bed.

"Okay now get up and freshen up, its 11.00", I said as if I was her hostel warden and I had to command her.

"Okay baby", she said as a romantic kid

"I will call you after my class", I said

"Okay but I need a kiss now, my good morning kiss", she said with a bit of shyness and more of naughtiness

"Baby, I can't I am in the class room", I said as I tried to avoid giving the kiss

"Noooooooo…" She said forcing my emotions

"Please baby", I tried hard to insist but it was really difficult to handle my sleeping beauty especially when she was on the bed. I had to kiss her as all my insistence had failed.

As soon as I kissed Salu all the girls in the class room started focusing at me as if I had raped one of them in the class room. I don't understand why girls love to be kissed in the presence of the general public by her partner. But if they are asked to kiss someone over the phone when they are in a public place they always have a hundred reasons for which they can't kiss you.

The classes were over and Mayank was at the gate to receive me. I went into the car shutting the door and disconnecting myself from the outer embarrassments. I narrated the whole story about the sleeping donkey of the class to all the members of the group as we reached to our so called picnic spot. Everyone had a hearty laugh other than me. Still the title of the sleeping donkey was revolving round my head. Later I gave an account of what had happened, to Salu commencing from the titles I had obtained in the whole day till the reactions of the girls when I had kissed her over the phone. We had a deal of narrating the whole days experience to each other at the end of the day. And one of the phone network's STD night packs had helped me to save a lot of my money over phone by then. She had laughed her lungs out but from the very day she had ensured I had gone to bed by 1.00 am at out of it by 6.00 am in the morning. Even though it would take me sixty to seventy calls to get up she had no negative reactions. And sometimes I would get up after her hundredth missed call but I had never seen her getting angry with me or scolding me for being late to receive her call. She would just give me my good morning kiss as soon as I got up and asked me to get ready for my college.

* * * *

Salu always had a habit of using some complicated English words while sending the text messages especially when I didn't receive her calls. Some of them were such I could not get it at the first sight. I had to read them twice or thrice to get the complete meaning of them. Some of them were too long to fit into the screen of one message file. So she used to send one message in two message files. But I loved to read those messages again and again when I missed her. Some of them brought tears in my eyes and some made me laugh. But I was really amazed about her English vocabulary at such a young age.

"Hey Prince, your image has captured my diverging thoughts. I have been vexed and worried for past few hours. What predicament of nature is this that does not allow the meeting of two lovers?" She used the word vexed but I had never seen her with any such expressions

"I have been lying in torpor in deep contemplation and cogitation of you baby….please reply…."

"Passing of every moment it feels my heart is slowing down. The surrounding is bulking my head with negative feelings and that is making

me sulkier. Please receive my call no" I loved the way she used the word no at the end of her statement.

"I hope you can understand the pain I am undergoing due to our separation. Please Prince Reply... For it is the only these saint hopes lingering in my mind over which I am surviving.... I only wish you reply soon baby.... I love my naughty boy."

* * * *

Chapter - 14

"I am going to drown. This global economical downfall is going to break my backbone dude" Mayank said with wrinkles on his fore head. We were sitting in front of his laptop and having a review on the share market. The prices of the share were going down. The value of the real estate were also drowning due to the global economical down fall.

"Don't worry dude, it's going to be all right within some days" I tried to console him but I was literally unsuccessful in doing so.

"I want to prove myself and I don't want my Dad and Mom's soul to repent for giving birth to a son like me." He said and I could see pain in his eyes.

A couple of years back Mayank had lost both his parents in a road accident. His Dad was a successful real estate business man. Mayank thought the road accident was a planned murder by some of his dad's business rivals. Mayank took the challenge of taking up the business at the age of sixteen with the help of some of his cousins. He separated his cousins from the business as soon as he turned eighteen because he could smell something fishy in the way of their working. He wanted to prove his dad's rival that they had to face him after his dad. He took up the business very successfully and everything was going on well before the global economical downfall started touching India's real estate market. Jobs were not available in the market. Many triumphant business men were ruined. Mayank still managed doing well as he was really affluent. He had invested a large amount of his cash in share market and the sensex had a heavy downfall. So he had to wait for a long for them to recover.

After the death of his parents Mayank had become very rough. He had too many cases lodged against his name in the police stations for washing his hand on people. He didn't have patience to listen to any one. He believed in achieving things through violence but he alone cannot be blamed for his behavior. He had become very revengeful after his dad's death. He wanted to find his parent's murderers and punish them. He was searching for them, like a hungry lion for its food.

Along with a successful business man he managed to become a well known negative figure in the nearby places. The cops didn't dare to do much if Mayank's name was involved in any of the activities. Everyone in our group soon became well known in the area. The cops started saluting all of us. No one dared to have a fight with us. In other words we had become dangerous criminals but we always supported the truth. Mayank used to keep a revolver for his protection. Sometimes he used it for fleeing away the goons. Any problems in our area were preferred to be brought in front of us rather than the police. The honest people loved our presence but the dishonest ones ran away from us.

Mayank believed in helping the poor people. So twice in a month he used to visit different slums in the city and provide them with some food stuffs. He also used to solve various problems there. He had literally become their God. He had become the final jury for the problems in the slums. His decisions were the final ones. People started trusting him more than the police and the corrupt politicians. Any problems occurred anywhere, Mayank was the first person informed before the police control room. Mayank always said "Money is not important in life; you need to have a heart to win the hearts of the people." He had actually won the hearts of thousands of people all around. Some used the term "criminal" for him but many others used the term "saviour". Any person who came to him with a request never went back empty handed. Indeed he had a colossal heart which was always ready to help others. For me he was a saviour to the people. He could not be called a criminal. I agree, he took the path of violence to achieve something good for the people but he never committed any crime.

And now the saviour was in great trouble due to the economical downfall. He didn't have much cash in his account. All of our group members started working together to revive him from his condition. It took a long time to recover from the loss but finally we were successful in our efforts. It is well said "Tolerance is the precious lubricant that keeps all our work very smooth and friction free."

Some of the people whom Mayank had helped in the past had also lent their hand for helping him. I could even see many people of the slums where Mayank used to visit. They were working for him without taking their daily wages on the construction sites of his real estate business. When I enquired about that with some of them, they said, "It's never fair to take something from God when he has given us so much in the past. We want to see him flying higher in the sky." I was very impressed with whatever they were doing for my friend. Reshma was a great help in our project of establishing Mayank's business position back to normal. She belonged to a business family so some of her tactful business tricks worked very well to attain the original position of the business in the society. By this time a good chemistry had been bucked up between Mayank and Reshma.

"Dude the share prices are raising at a great speed and the business has also recovered a lot" Mayank shouted with pleasure as we were relaxing in his place. He was as usual busy with his laptop. Sometimes he behaved like typical businessmen. Every one of us was very happy. But the happiest person I could find was Reshma. She had a big smile on her face.

"This calls for a party" Rohan said as he was all time ready for a party, a visit to a disco or a drink at any time of the day. If he was asked to have beer instead of his bed tea he would gladly accept the offer.

"Yes, we need to celebrate and I am going to sponsor it this time", Reshma said

"But….." Mayank tried to speak but Reshma injected him.

"I am going to throw the party tonight" Reshma said without looking at Mayank's face.

"No queries please" she said avoiding Mayank's face. Mayank could just smile at the situation. Something was striking my brain even though Mayank had not spoken anything like that to me. He had just said that Reshma and he were having long chats at the late hours of night.

We had a grand celebration at Reshma's place with drinks, dinner and lots of fun. Reshma's parents were out that night so we had a blast. The only thing which I was missing was Salu's presence. I really missed her during the party hours. But I followed the trick she had taught me when I had expressed this to her. She had said "open the gallery of your phone, then open my photo and kiss me." That always did the trick for me. I felt good and relaxed once I had performed the act.

* * * *

A letter from Salu:

My Honey,

Today finally I have decided to open up a little and pen down a pool of feelings for my shona from the waves of thoughts in the ocean of my mind. It has become hard for me to ignore this love, so intense that I feel for you.

I always wished I would express my feelings and thoughts for you that rose from the depths of my heart and mind in person holding you in my warm arms and gazing into your passionate eyes. But our physical separation by the miles of emptiness has made it impossible for me at this moment. Sometimes, I have told myself that there is no room for you and me because we are a world apart. However, I cannot deny deep inside my heart, I am hoping for the two of us. Before when I had no special love in my life, I always envied hearing to my friends' life of love and planned how I would talk, how I would react to different situations and how I would express my feelings etc. to my beloved. But today when I have already stepped into my love life and want to do those things, I am just lost.

I never imagined the 1st man in my life I would love so very much, who would possess such a prominent place of my life, who would become the apple of my eye, would come to me under such circumstances. Like a thread binds the beads in a necklace, your innate beauty binds your lovable personality. Your unusual simplicity and masculine qualities have always filled my mind with ecstasy. You came into my life as a gentle soothing breeze blowing over me. You are the person who taught me how to love and explained me the meaning of love. You have showed me such a charming side of life with full of happiness and hope that I have started loving it more as never before. Now I want my life to be eternal. I want to spend every second of my life with you, make every moment an intimate one. Do not want to miss any expression on your face may it be of love, anger, hope, happiness, grief, etc. I doubt whether a future heaven would be more pleasant and sweet as the present is, with the delicate company of yours.

Sometimes when my mind reads fast all the moments spent with you since our 1st meeting till date and I relive some of the past happenings, am not able to believe and explain it to my heart that, Yes, I am in love..... You are the only person with whom I have shared both a laughter and a tear within such a short period of time.

The drives we went for sightseeing and those small moments we spent together during the journey, the way your slightest touch made me feel out of world will always be cherished as the best times of life. I can still feel the coldness in my body, every time I relive the moment when you threw some snow balls on me which ran down my body through my cleavage sensing goose bumps. As we spent more time together, the thorn of love pierced my heart deeper and the pain of staying away from you grew.

And how can I forget the time when I was separated from my family due to the internal fights and you stood beside me consoling. It was only your words and undying faith at that moment that kept the hope of getting back my family alive in me. Now, I realize how you would be also feeling when we were shut in the shop and your heart would be beating faster as mine but you never made me realize the same. I love you so much.....my baby....

Now, let me tell you about the loveliest moments of my life. It was when we spent time together in my hotel room in the last night before we left Kashmir. My words will always fall short in order to describe that moment. Your idea of having romance and sharing some sensual words in dim light with soft music can never be put to words. It can just be felt. I really miss that tender kiss of yours on my forehead, the passionate one on the left side of my neck, your love bite in my right ear and most touchingly your sensual kiss on my lips. When our lips were locked, it seemed as if they were whispering into each other's ear and sucking our hearts. It was like rising of two waves in the tides of love, breaking and meeting at the beach of lips. It was like two loves leaving their homes for an unknown land; seem to have met at the body's limit, at the confluence of their lips. Your lustrous budding lips and sparkling eyes always flashes in the screen of my mind.

I miss you very much dear. I miss your smile that conceals the fragrance and secret of your love. I am not able to bear this distance anymore. Your separation from me incinerates my whole body like a fire of my desire which can be extinguished only with your splash of love....

After your departure, I am hallucinating. Wherever I open my eyes your face appears to me. You are always in my mind by the time I wake up till I close my eyes. I feel so lifted each time I think about you. I am missing you like crazy darling and I feel I will go mad. Each moment I think about you lasts like an hour and an hour like a day as I am away from you. Every night I long for the sensual passion of your kisses and comfort of your hug. Your thoughts give warm to my cold lonely nights. I cannot bear the emptiness created in my vicinity after you have left. I want to meet you soon, honey. Come to me. I want to hug you tight and be lost in your embrace hearing to your precious heartbeats. At last I want to say, I am always yours and you are mine. I love you my prince.......

Your sweet baby Angel,

Salu

* * * *

Chapter - 15

"Mom please, I want to have paneer today", I said

"No, you have to take boiled vegetables", mom commanded as we were in the kitchen. I felt I was with Sweety. Both had the same habit of commanding without taking the consent of the person in front of them.

"Mom, come on it's a Sunday", I tried to convince her

"Sunday, so what?", she said

"Please prepare something special for your only son." I tried hard to blackmail her emotionally but everything went in vain. I had forgotten that Hitler rule was over but it still existed in our house especially when it is related to balanced diet and my mom.

"No I don't want to make my only son, a fatso!" she replied

"OKAY!!!!!! Prepare whatever you want" I spoke with a bit of frustration and swift out of the kitchen to switch on the television. The only thing I found worthy enough to watch was the commencing India-England one day match with Shewag smashing the ball all round the ground. Or else the television channels were full of daily soaps intending more for the house wives. I don't know how they manage to elongate the stories. Some of the stories last for more than a thousand episodes creating a boredom but the Indian house wives manage well to cope with them in their pace. May be that's the reason television is called an idiot box. Soon Shewag was bowled out breaking my hopes like glass slab. I switched off the idiot box and ran to my room to absorb my frustration.

I was missing something from the morning. I started thinking with my physics notes in my hand, resting my body on my cosy bed. Suddenly I remembered, I had to wake up Salu. It was Sunday and it was my turn to wake her up. We had a pact, the whole week she took the charge of waking me up and on Sunday I had to wake her up. And it was already 10.00 and I had not called her yet. I immediately jumped over my phone and dialed her number and as soon as she picked up the call

"Good morning my sweet angel, I am sorry", I apologized for calling her late as a kid for not completing his homework

"My good morning kiss please", She said with a sleepy voice. She was still on her bed may be waiting for my call. The only thing I had been marking that she never missed her good morning kiss even though she was very stressed up.

"My lovely Angel", I said and kissed her

"That's like my naughty boy", she said and kissed in return. In no circumstances she failed to use the word naughty boy for me at least once a day. It sounded good to me.

"Are you still on bed?" I asked in surprise as she always left bed before six unless we had a long night talk session or if she had some assignments to complete.

"Yes, I was waiting for your call", she said happily without any amount of anger flashing from her voice for not waking her up early.

"Okay, then freshen up and text me", I said

"Ok honey", she said and hung up.

I could only complete half my physics notes before my mom called me downstairs to engulf the tasteless boiled vegetables with pepper and salt. I had no other option. I wanted to throw them down. But it was just next to impossible. My diet concerned mom stood next to me like a jailer, to make sure that I didn't throw her beloved boiled vegetables into the dustbin. I completed my lunch as a school going kid. I was then directed by my mom to get ready for visiting the exhibition ground for some handloom expo. I wasn't interested and we had a long argument. The debate extended for an hour or may be more but finally as usual I had to give up and work as per her direction. An immediate thought that stroke my brain was the huge amount of similarities of Mom and Sweety of imposing decision on others. "HANDLOOM EXPO", the name itself sounded so old fangled. I felt as if some pre eminent power forced me to wear an antiquated pair of clothes. I felt handloom expos were meant for grey haired people and for people like us in our salad ages are meant for auto expos. I was getting ready when my phone beeped with the arrival of a text message.

"What's my Prince doing????" It was Salu. Her message's arrival was the only good thing that happened to me after my lunch. I felt as if someone had provided me with oxygen in Deep Ocean.

"Your mom-in-law is pulling your Prince to visit an oldie type Handloom expo", I replied

"Wow!!!!! Then you must visit and bring something for me" she replied

"Please baby!!! I will be bored there", I replied

"Don't worry I am there no", she replied and I loved it. Even though she was hundreds of kilometres away from me, I knew she was there with me anytime and every time. She never let me the geographical distance disturb our love.

After a chat session with my sweetheart I moved down the stairs dragging my feet as a reluctant kid. As soon as I reached the door of my parents' room I saw my mom dressed up in the salwar suit which Salu had gifted her. I loved it. She looked so pretty in them. May be because it was gifted by Salu it seemed more beautiful to my eyes.

"Wow mom you are looking great", I said

"Obviously it is my son's gift", she said and I felt guilty of not telling her about Salu.

We immediately packed ourselves in the car and set for the handloom expo. It took us half an hour to reach the expo ground. On our way we had a prolonged discussion about my gift which was actually Salu's gift. As soon as we reached I could see only middle aged aunties and uncles all around. There were only a handful of youngsters my eyes could catch hold of, who probably came in groups to kill their time or to spend some time with their girlfriends away from home. I felt lonely. I thought I could be with my group and enjoy my life instead. My cell phone beeped

"Has my Janu baby reached the expo" Salu had sent.

"Yes, and he is surrounded by thousand of sexy looking aunties", I replied with an intension of teasing her

"Dare not he looks at one of those thousands aunties", she replied filled with jealousy. I was now fond of her jealousy filled statements.

"Mom is wearing your gift today and I feel so guilty", I replied.

"Wow!!!! But why are you feeling guilty", she replied.

"Because I haven't told her about you and she thinks it's my gift", I tried to express my guilt.

"We both are one. So who ever gifts her it's the same na, baby", She replied and I was so impressed at her matured way of handling situations. She was trying to drive me away from the delinquent feeling and at the same time she expressed her love for me.

"I love you baby... and mom is looking really cute in her new attire." I replied as she completely cooled me down

"She is our mom. She has to look cute." She replied and the word ***our*** used by her soaked my heart. She always used our mom and our dad instead of your mom, your dad, my mom and my dad. Sometimes I felt I was only elder to her by age but she was a lot elder to me by her maturity and love for me and both the families.

We went around the stalls and I purchased a ladies cell phone holder for Salu. She could hang it round her neck and put the cell phone in it. I had to hide my gift before mom could locate it and start her crime branch type investigation on the expo ground. After a lot of shopping from the expo, mom finally decided to spare me by leaving the ground filled with oldies.

* * * *

Chapter - 16

"Happy birthday Prince", Salu said.

"Thank you baby", I said. She had called exactly at 12.00 am as she wanted to be the first person to wish me my birthday. And she became the first person to wish me. I wanted the selfsame, so I tried to keep my phone free from other calls. We had a chat of around fifteen minutes. I almost had fifteen missed calls from my friends during the call. I knew I was going to be thrashed by my friends on receiving their calls.

After my chat with Salu my phone rang with the name flashing Mayank. I received the call with a fear of getting a heavy scolding.

"Happy birthday to our hero" came almost five to six voices together. I was surprised. All my close ones were waiting for me to pick their call in a conference calling. It included Mayank, Neel, Rohan, Aditi, Raghav and Sweety.

"Thank you dear", I said as I was so happy to be wished by all of them all together.

"Hey we want you to take Salu to the conference call", Rohan said

"And Minti too", Mayank insisted as I could understand his intensions well. But I could not tell "no" at least today. So I brought in all of them into the conference call and nine of us had a chat of around three hours. It was lovely. I did not care for anyone else wishing me when my friends and my love were with me. I could not express the amount of happiness I had received that day.

"Happy birthday", my mom said hugging me. I touched her feet to take her blessings to start another year of my life, expecting it to be successful.

"Happy birthday", my dad wished as I took his blessings caressing his feet. Many calls came from my relatives wishing me my birthday.

The morning was fantastic. I loved it.

"Hey what's the matter why are you bringing me here?" I asked as Mayank dragged me into a restaurant. I was completely uninformed about what was happening.

"Wait for a minute you will come to know everything", He said. As we were moving towards a cabin of the restaurant which was dark I didn't have any idea what was happening. As I stepped in the lights came up suddenly with the bursting of a balloon. I could see the beautifully decorated cabin with my full gang present there. They started singing the birthday song in unison with Raghav playing his harmonica. I was spellbound. I didn't know what should be my reaction at the moment. My mouth was wide open. I put my hand over my mouth to avoid the entry of any pest. The cabin was very delicately decorated with bi coloured balloons i.e. blue and white. As Mayank knew it well that blue was my favourite colour. Indeed the cabin looked splendid. I was informed that all the decorations were done by Mayank and Rohan with their full effort of three long hours. They had arranged for a big black forest cake with dark chocolates on it with *HAPPY BIRTHDAY GYAN* engraved using white cream. I felt on the top of the world. The table was decorated with my favourite beer bottles in a pyramid structure. It was glamorous. I definitely wanted to have a go at once but my promise to my sweetheart restricted me doing that.

"Won't you have a drink", Rohan asked looking at me with playful eyes.

"No, I won't you may have one dude", I said

"Why!!!!!!!!", Neel was shocked

"I have promised Salu that I will not touch alcohol", I said with a childish voice

"Come on it's your birthday", Raghav insisted

"I will just come back", Mayank said and moved out of the cabin as I kept strongly to my statement. The rest of them started preparing for the cutting of the cake and the grand party. Suddenly my cell phone rang flashing Salu on it.

"Hello baby", I said

"Hello my naughty birthday boy", she said with a playful voice

"Do you know something; these people had arranged a surprise birthday party for me", I said with excitement

"Yes dear I know, Neel had called me this morning. She told me everything about the surprise." she elaborated

"You knew all about this and you didn't tell me!!" I asked for a justification

"Surprises are not to be opened before time; and one more thing is that you have the permission to have a drink today" she said as I was jerked by her statement. I had never asked for any permission. I hadn't even spoken a single word to her about the well enriched beer bottles.

"Thank you dear, but how did you come to know about this", I had a mixed feeling of being happy as well as I was surprised about the fact.

"Everything cannot be disclosed my dear and remember you have the permission only for today, Bye", she said and hung up.

We were ready for the cutting the cake but I was missing the organizer of the party. Mayank had gone out and yet not come in. I asked Rohan to go out and pull Mayank in. We could start the party as soon as possible on Mayank's arrival. As he was stepping out in search of Mayank I could see Mayank coming in. He came without giving any justifications for his moving out. He sat on the chair beside me.

"Did you get the permission for your drink today?" he asked in my ear not letting anyone else hear our conversation and smiled at me. It was again another surprising fact for me in the day. Now I could understand the reason before Salu's approval for the drink. He had called her up and convinced her for the drinks party. I was speechless; I could only look at him and smile back. I hugged him tight.

"Thank you so much bro", I said

In the evening I spent some time with my parents as we went to the pizza hut to celebrate my birthday with a variety of pizzas. It was the best birthday of my life. I was feeling as if I was on cloud nine. I could never have such a brilliant birthday ever in my life without all of my much-loved buddies, my parents and my sweetheart.

* * * *

Chapter - 17

“Hurry up Gyan, we need the blood immediately”, Mayank shouted as I was trying to start my motor bike.

“This bloody bike always gives a problem!!”, I said and punched the fuel tank with anger and hope that it would start. Although I had hurt my hand, my hopes had come true with powerful kick.

Neel had faced a severe accident with a Maruti van and she was admitted in Kalinga hospital in Bhubaneswar. She was kept in the Intensive care unit. We needed blood before the docs could start the operation. None of our group members had the same blood group as hers. It was a rare blood group i.e. AB negative. Mayank and I belonged to the O positive group. Sweety and Rohan were of “A” negative group. Raghav and Aditi belonged to the “B” positive group. It was absolutely disastrous not to have any one around us to help us. We were trying to reach all our contacts for the blood group but it was just worthless. We couldn’t find any one with the same blood group. So we decided to exchange blood in the blood bank and get the necessary amount of blood for Neel. All had tears in their eyes. It was tough to think anything other than our sweet darling’s recovery. She was a sweetheart to all of us. But Raghav had decided to smash the driver of the Maruti Van who had caused the disaster for us. He had even enquired the residential address of the person through the RTO officials. He was just waiting for the recovery of Neel.

I drove the bike with more than the speed of 120 to reach Cuttack, the so called twin city of the capital city of Odisha. It had the best blood bank in the whole state. We had to exchange two bottles of our blood for two bottles of AB negative blood. That means Mayank and I had to give our blood. We lay down on the bed as per the medical assistant’s command. Mayank was lying down on the bed left of mine.

“Is it your first time?” Mayank asked

“Yes, and what about you?” I replied

“Same here” he said

“Are you afraid?” I asked

"Not at all, anything for our sweet darling" he said and the medical assistant pierced the needle into our vein handing each one of us with a sponge ball to keep a uniformity in the flow of blood. It took us just ten minutes to give our blood. Then after some formalities we were provided with two bottles of AB negative blood. It was now time for us to drive back. Now the speed of the bike rose to more than 150 and it just took us ten odd minutes to cover the distance of thirty kilo meters from Cuttack to Bhubaneswar.

We reached the hospital where Neel was admitted and handed over the bottles of blood to the hospital representative. They started the preparation for the operation. Neel was transferred to the operation theatre. Soon the operation commenced and all of us had our fingers crossed. I informed Salu about the situation, she was worried. She busted out crying over the phone as both of them had become very close friends. But I managed to handle her emotions with a lot of hard work. My next job was to call Minti and ask her to control her sister. By the time I completed all this stuff, I could see the doctor moving out of the operation theatre. All of us ran towards him to know the status.

"How is she now?" Sweety asked with her eyes filled with tears. I took her into my arms to control her vehemence.

"The operation was successful, but………" the doctor said but he was interrupted by Raghav

"But what doctor?" he almost shouted in a very terrified voice, which must have troubled the other patients of the hospital but his sentiments were justified.

"But you have to wait for two to three hour for her to come back to her senses", the doctor said and all of us looked up thanking the almighty to save our sweet friend from such a severe accident. No one had even taken a sip of water since the morning. So I decided to bring in some food for everyone. I took some biscuits and bread for everyone but none of us could swallow anything. I called Salu to inform her that the operation was successful. Minti informed me that she was in the temple and promised not to come back till Neel had regained consciousness. I was touched. After a long wait of two hours the nurse came out of the intensive care unit to inform us that she was back to her senses and we could meet her. It had become the best news delivered to us by anyone in the whole year. These two hours were like two years for everyone around. My heart was almost in my mouth in these two long hours.

"Hey how is our sweet candy", Rohan said as we entered the I.C.U. Neel was on her bed looking at us with wide eyes. She had broken her left hand in the accident so the plaster was on. She gave a sweet smile as we entered. Sweety held her hand as few drops went down her eyes. Neel was looking at the door again and again. She was waiting for someone. She fired the question at us to which no one of us had any answer.

"Did you try to contact Dad?" She asked as all of us looked at each other's face. None of us had enough courage to tell anything to her.

"Yes, Neel we tried but could not reach him", Raghav tried to manage but she understood it well.

"Yes, I know Raghav, you don't have to justify. He must be busy", she said and a long silence prevailed in the unit.

Neel had left her house almost before three years. After her mom's death, her dad got married to another lady who was very mean with her. So after her tenth she left her house and started living in a rented house. Her dad was a successful business man. He sent a heavy amount of money to her daughter every month, but had never called her or tried to meet her since then. We had tried to reach him after Neel's accident. He said he was busy and he could not come. He had said any requirement of money would be sent by him, but we didn't feel like taking his help. We were self sufficient to save our sweet little baby without his money. I never understood why people always compared relationships with money in this century. Raghav tried to manage when she asked about her dad but Neel knew her dad more than any one of us.

"Hey, can I get a mirror please", Neel asked may be she was trying to adjust the situation.

"Why do you need a mirror now? We are not going for a party." Rohan said with a shocking expression

"Get it first for me" she said as Rohan ran out to get it for her. As soon as he came back she snatched the mirror from him and started looking at her face.

"Thank God!!!!! My face has not been damaged" she shouted. I never understood why girls always cared about their faces more than anything else. A girl who has seven stitches on her head, plasters on her left hand and undergone a serious surgery before few hour was happy because no damage was done to her face!! It was completely out of my imagination. Girls are absolutely difficult objects to understand, made by God.

I called Salu and both Neel and Salu had a chat of almost twenty minutes before the doctors restricted her from talking so much. They advised her to take rest. We were told to move outside the cabin. In the next few days everything was back to normal and Neel was discharged from the hospital. We had a grand celebration on her return from the hospital. But as promised by Raghav, he had smashed the driver of the Maruti Van and had admitted him in the intensive care unit of the same hospital where Neel was admitted. Mayank and Raghav always followed the principle of an eye for an eye.

* * * *

Chapter - 18

25th of November - Salu's first birthday after coming into relationship with me

I dialled Salu's number at 11.00 pm. I wanted to talk to her before someone else could wish her before me. I waited for the clock to strike 12.00 midnight.

"Happy birthday to my sweet Angel", I said and she seemed very happy.

"Thank you, the prince of my life. You are the first one to wish me", she said,

"Obviously and keep it in your mind that I am always going to be the first one to wish you on all your birthdays", I said,

"Is it?" she asked with a voice trying to tease me.

"Do I need to give a clarification?" I asked

"No need I can trust you more than I trust myself my dear prince" she said and I could feel the trust in her voice.

"Okay now talk to others. I am sure you must have missed many calls by now" I said

"Yes, Mayank bhaiya, Neel di and many others have been calling me since long", she said

"I love you and many many happy returns of the day. I promise you that I will be there with you on your next birthday. We are going to celebrate it in a grand way." I said and hung up. I am sure, she was very happy listening to the last statement of mine.

The next day early in the morning I received a call from Mayank. He asked me for a treat. I could not disagree. After all it was Salu's birthday. I threw up a party in a restaurant nearby. I had ordered for a dark chocolate cake, Salu's favourite flavour. The tables were full of all kind of wine. I tried to make the decoration more elegant than the decorations on my birthday party.

Everyone had a good enjoyment. We called Salu from the restaurant and she badly wanted to be a part of the party. I even wanted that, but I knew it was not possible. It had become a special day for me. I never felt her absence. She was omnipresent. Everywhere I went she went with me. Everything I did, I took her advice and she would give me advice which always proved cent percent correct.

The foremost things were I was never able to tell a lie to her. Any time I tried to speak one she would catch me by my style of speaking. Whenever I missed my mom and dad I used to call her and she understood before I could tell her anything. I was too lucky to have someone like her in my life.

* * * *

Chapter - 19

"What am I going to do? He wants to come back to my life. But I can't trust him anymore", Sweety said as we were resting in Reshma's place. Ronny, Sweety's ex-boy friend had met her a day back and asked her to come back in a relationship. They had a break up long back due to the disloyal nature of Ronny.

"Just listen to your heart and take a decision, and don't let him force his decision on you", Reshma advised. I felt it was really sensible piece of advice at the point of time.

Sweety had left her home years back due to her father's habit of over consumption of alcohol. His father used to drink a lot and then charge at her and her mother. Her mother was a simple lady so she didn't dare to raise her voice against her husband. Sweety became frustrated. She left her home when she was in seventh grade and started staying with her aunt. She started hating her father for his drunkenness and her mother for keeping quiet. But I have seen the pain in her eyes at times of getting separated from her parents. She had never contacted them after she left her house. They had tried to come in touch with her but she didn't care to respond. After she successfully cleared her tenth grade examinations she took up a job in a call centre and stayed with Aditi and Neel in their rented room. She managed her daily expenses and studies with the job she took up.

She had met Ronny when she was in tenth grade. They soon came into a relationship. The relationship lasted for six months before Mayank came up with some instances of Ronny's disloyalty towards Sweety. Sweety broke up with Ronny and started hating love. She didn't want to fall in love with anyone.

But two days back Ronny met Sweety and asked her to forgive him. Mayank didn't want her to fall into the same ditch again and dirty her clothes. So he spoke strictly against the guy.

"I don't want you to come in any relationship with him", Mayank spoke very strongly.

"I don't have any interest but something is hurting my heart since I have meet him last" Sweety tried to explain her feeling but Mayank was not ready to listen to any explanation of her.

"Stop it dear. Let her speak her heart out" Reshma requested Mayank.

"I just don't want to listen to any of her feelings which involves that idiot" Mayank spoke aiming at Ronny.

"Okay, if you say so I don't care for that guy" Sweety said with her numbed eyes looking at Mayank.

"You have your friends to care for you dear", Mayank said trying to justify his words.

"I don't care for anyone if you all are with me", Sweety spoke. Mayank hugged her tight. I could see a deviating pain in her eyes which cannot be expressed in mere words.

"This calls for a party" Rohan said as this was always his usual statement after any problem of our group was sorted out.

"Idiot don't you have any other suggestion" Neel shouted at him and all of us had a hearty laugh. But Sweety's eyes were still numbed.

"I am going to throw the party tonight" Mayank said with a monumental smile looking at Sweety. He was very happy for her and her decision. She smiled back. But I still felt there was something wrong.

We had a party that night. Mayank's party always had all kinds of alcohols in it. You can always find the best quality alcohol ever present with him. I could see Sweety's face tensed. She was giving fake smiles. I went to her and sat beside her with my glass of soft drinks.

"Are you not happy with the decision you took this morning?" I asked without looking at her.

"No dear, I don't have any problem with the decision", she said trying to hide her emotions.

"Then why are you upset?" I asked.

"I am missing my parents a lot. If they would have been with me then I would not need the support of fools like Ronny", she said and I could feel an intense and a conflicting pain in very voice. I took out my cell phone and handed it over to Sweety. She could not understand what I was doing.

"Dial the number", I said

"Whose number should I dial?" She asked, her voice full of confusion

"Your Dad's" I said and there was a non identical silence between us. The silence always meant a positive reaction sometimes. So I believed to take the silence in a positive way. She wanted to talk to her dad but could never express it to anyone.

"What?? Are you crazy?" she spoke trying to pretend that she was not interested to talk to her Dad but her eyes gave discrepant reactions. The only thing I could do was to force her.

"Yes, I have gone crazy and I want you to talk to your dad" I shouted just to show her that I meant it and it was nothing wrong. All the eyes were on us. Rohan felt safe to switch off the music system.

"I haven't talked to him since the last four years. I don't know whether he remembers me or not" she said and her statement made me more positive about the step I was taking.

"He is your Dad dear and parents always love their kids. They can never forget their children!!" I spoke as I went close to her holding her hand, showing a bit of affection.

"Please dear. At least do it for me. Please", I continued as she took the phone in her hand. Her habit of ordering things didn't work in front of her emotions. She dialed the number gathering all her courage. Someone picked up the call. After a few moments of silence,

"Dad" Sweety spoke as her eyes were wet. She had a conversation. I could not hear the conversation of the other side, but what I predicted from the side I could hear was it was going on really good. Subsequently the telephonic conversation was over and tears ran down her cheeks. I got up from my seat without speaking a word. Neel went to her and hugged her tight. I was moving out of the room.

"Gyan" Sweety called me from behind. I turned back to listen.

"Thank you so much", she said with a smile and pearls still rolling down her eyes. I just smiled back at her and moved away from the hall.

She visited her parents the next day. She seemed very happy after that. Her father promised her that he will get admitted in a rehabilitation centre and stop drinking. But she didn't want to be away from the group so she decided to stay with Neel and Aditi. She visited her parents regularly thereupon. All the sour feelings were omitted between the father and the daughter.

* * * *

Chapter - 20

1st of April, 2010 after one year - Our first Anniversary

"Come on Gyan we are getting late for the flight", Mayank shouted. We had planned a day's visit to Rajasthan for celebrating my one year successful relationship with Salu. Mayank and I had to fly to Rajasthan. I wanted to surprise Salu. I had asked Minti to help me in my surprise. Our flight was going to land in Rajasthan at 10.00 in the morning and the next day I had to fly back to Bhubaneswar at 11.00 am. I had told mom that I was going to stay in my friend's house for the night.

"Yes dude just a minute", I said

"You are always a late latif. Your physics lecturer was not wrong calling you a sleeping donkey." Mayank shouted at me when I moved out of the house. Probably, he was trying to remind me of my past embarrassments. He always loved to do it and make me feel guilty.

All my group members had come to drop us in the Bhubaneswar airport. We reached the Rajasthan airport at 10.00 am. I could see Salu and Minti from a distance. I had not received Salu's call since last night. She had messaged me her good wishes for our anniversary. I knew she was upset, as her crying smileys in the messages depicted the amount of sadness. I had asked Minti to bring her to the airport. And she had done it successfully.

I went close to them but she did not care to look up. She was busy with her cell phone. May be she was trying to call me as I could feel my phone vibrating in my pocket. I hugged her with a surprise. She shouted thinking that some outsider had hugged her. Even some of the airport securities were almost ready to pounce on me for her protection. But when her eyes fell on my face she was mesmerized. She could not believe her eyes. She thought maybe it was her illusion.

"Happy anniversary baby" I said, as she still had her hands covering her mouth which had opened to a great extent due to over excitement.

"Happy anniversary", she said and hugged me hard as the airport security personals were staring at us as if they were fooled on the April fool day. We hired a cab to a hotel where Minti had already arranged for our stay.

"Di, why didn't you tell me about his visit?" Salu fired her queries at Minti

"Actually I had asked her to do the same. I wanted to surprise you. And you remember surprises are not to be revealed before time", I said without letting Minti answer and reminding her about the statement she gave during my birthday surprise.

"Pinch me. I still can't believe you are in Rajasthan and sitting beside me", she said looking at me.

"Is it?" I said and kissed her taking the benefit of Minti looking outside the window. But I could see the driver looking back at us through the mirror and smiling. But that moment I didn't have to care about the outsiders.

The hotel was far away from the airport but just at ten minutes walking distance from their house. Minti had done a good job. We reached the hotel and decided to go for lunch without freshening up. The only day I had was 1st of April. I didn't want to waste a single minute. I still remembered the day I proposed to her on the snow. I still remembered the way she reacted. I still remembered the day completely! It was a high definition video in my memory.

As soon as we reached the restaurant I took out the dark chocolate cake which was my sweetheart's favourite. It was heart shaped. I had engraved HAPPY ANNIVERSARY MY DEAR ANGEL on it which made her happy. She became blissful looking at the cake. I took out some more gifts for her from my baggage. I had taken a white long skirt and a white top for her. She looked like a cute angel in white so I preferred to see her in white every time. I had always visualized her in white. She was very gratified receiving the gifts. And finally I took out the mobile holder which I had bought for her from the handloom expo and the card for her in which I had written how much I loved her. Although I could never express my feelings only with a pen and a piece of paper but I had tried my level best to do as much as I could. We had our lunch completely according to my favourite dishes as per Salu's wish and I could not dare to deny her wishes.

After lunch we went to the hotel to freshen up. Minti promised me that she would be in the hotel by 4.00 pm along with Salu. I didn't want to leave her, but the strict face of the idli sick idiot constrained on me to allow her to move to her home. We had decided to visit a fort in Jodhpur and then have our dinner together.

"This is a brilliant monument" Mayank spoke as we were moving around in the fort.

"Yes this was made before six hundred years by a very powerful king to get protected from his enemies" Minti said giving as much knowledge as she had about the fort.

"I want to be as rich as the kings of those days." Mayank said closing his eyes and then looking up to the sky. May be he was dreaming about the kings or maybe he was praying to God for making him rich.

"Sir, please come back to the reality. We are in Rajasthan now and tomorrow morning we are going to fly back to Bhubaneswar", I said and I could see Salu's face drowning. I knew she didn't like the last statement of mine. But that was the reality. I had to return. I embraced her to chill her. It was our anniversary and I didn't want her to be upset.

The fort visit was over and we had our dinner in the hotel. Mayank and Minti decided to give us some lone time in the room. They went for a walk and Minti allotted a time limit of an hour as her usual habit of allotting time. As soon as Minti and Mayank moved out of the room I went to Salu and slept on her lap. She moved her hand and I could feel the intimate love from her which I missed every time. We had only an hour before Minti and Mayank could come into the room.

Salu switched on the music system which played soft bollywood music. The soft music and the dim light of the room had started its effect on both of us. Our lips came close to each other. Within no time they came in touch. We kissed each other very passionately. Slowly my lips went down to her neck and then to her chest. I was mesmerized and a high voltage current passed through her body. My lips were busy kissing hers with my hands on her bosoms. She started unbuttoning my shirt and then completely removed it. My hands had become naughty enough to remove her top. We kissed each other wildly. My lips and hand became very busy with her boobs giving her the complete pleasure.

Suddenly the door bell rang and we had to wear our clothes without any delay. It was Mayank and Minti. The allotted one hour was over. I was sad. I wanted to live this hour of my life again and again. It was the first time we had an on-bed romance with each other. Both of us enjoyed it thoroughly. But we had to depart now. Mayank and I went on a walk with Minti and Salu to safely drop them in their house. Salu promised me that she will be there in the hotel with me early next morning. She kept her promise. She came to the hotel at 6.00 am after waking me up at 5.00 am. Minti and Salu both had huge boxes in their hands.

"What's that?" I asked in a surprise

“Breakfast for all of us prepared by chef Salu and chef Minti”, she said with a very jolly voice.

“Wow breakfast. I am very hungry” Mayank said and jumped up to the basket as if hc had not seen food since years.

Salu took out the food and served it in three plates. She had prepared parathas with extra pond of homemade ghee, paneer tikkas, toast and sweets. All were my favourite and I wanted to taste something prepared by my sweetheart. I tried to take a plate.

“Stop!!” Salu said to my shock as I banged the plate down with a stupor.

“What happened? Am I not allowed to eat?” I asked with a revolt.

“You are, but I have something else for us”, she said and took out a small box from the basket. She opened it. I could see parathas and toasts prepared in the shape of a heart. The toasts had LOVE YOU PRINCE written on them with tomato sauce. I didn’t want to eat them instead preserve them and keep looking at them. I could just smile at her. Words would never fit into the situation.

“Buddy you are going to enjoy a lot”, Mayank said with parathas stuffed in his mouth. I looked at him and asked him to explain the statement with our famous eye contact.

“She prepares food so well. I feel like biting my finger”, he continued and we had a good laugh.

We had to check out the hotel by 9.00 am so that we could catch our flight by 11.00 am. We reached the airport on time. Salu handed me over a wrist watch as my anniversary gift. It was lovely.

“Keep a track of the time looking at this watch and give me regular calls” she said as she handed me over the watch.

“Don’t I call you at regular intervals”, I said trying to make my voice naughty.

“But I need more frequent calls Prince” she said and hugged me before the last announcement was made for our flight. I didn’t want to leave. But I had to before mom got any hint about my single day trip to Rajasthan.

* * * *

Chapter - 21

"I am not able to take these responsibilities any more" Raghav spoke as we were peacefully resting under our usual picnic spot.

"Why do you get panic attacks dude", I said.

"No buddy it's becoming too much burden on me now" he said with his face dipping down in full of stressfulness.

"Just chill and let's see what can be done" Mayank said as he always had a solution to every problem whether it is appropriate for the person or not.

Raghav's dad was murdered by some of the land mafias before years. His mother committed suicide not able to tolerate the pain of her husband's death. Raghav was a good student so he decided to continue his studies as well as look after his dad's business. He was in seventh grade when he lost both his parents. So he made himself very strong and had the same revengeful nature as Mayank. He had a younger sister who had to be taken care of by him. He kept his younger sister as his daughter, giving her all the love that he never received from his parents.

He was the owner of ten trucks which earned him a good amount for his expenditure and over expenditure. Maximum of the trucks he rented, worked in Mayank's real estate business. He also owned five stores in some of the malls in Bhubaneswar. It was very difficult for him to manage those but somehow he managed them well.

Now that the pressures of studies were touching the skies it was troubling him. He was not able to manage all the work together. Even though we lent him a helping hand but he had decided to sell some of his stores. It would earn him a good deal. We were having a hot discussion of what can be done.

"Hey I have an idea" Mayank said and I had a doubt because all his ideas were always out of my imagination sometimes in such situations.

"What idea do you have now" Raghav asked and I could clearly see frustration bursting out of his voice.

"Why do you want to sell them to outsiders? Let me take over the stores and once your studies are completed you can take it back from me."

He said and I could sense something sensible this time from Baba Mayank Dev's solution box.

"Wow why didn't it strike to my mind?" Raghav said with excitement showing his acceptance to Mayank's idea.

"We are not going to need any paper work if we do that" Mayank said and the atmosphere was turning completely business type.

"But we need some trust worthy people to take care of the stores" Raghav said

"Yes we have two trust worthy and sexy girls who can take care of the stores and even attract customers" Mayank said pointing at Aditi and Sweety.

"What? Are you crazy? We are already into a job." Aditi said getting surprised at Mayank's offer.

"You are going to get double the amount of your present salary and most importantly can't you help your friend" he spoke trying to black mail them emotionally and to some extent bribing them with a higher salary package.

I knew the bribe would not work but the trap of emotional blackmailing worked well on both of them. Mayank was a perfect business man. He knew what to do in an imbalanced situation and balance it. Sweety and Aditi looked at each other's face and finally agreed to Mayank's offer. Now the stores were safe in his hands. He promised to return them to Raghav as soon as his studies were over.

"That calls…" Rohan tried to speak something but he was interrupted by Neel

"Yes, I knew you are going to speak now, after the problem was over and ask for a party" Neel said and everyone laughed. Rohan was dumped this time.

"He has a sense and we need a party. After all I need to be a bit relaxed" Raghav said and we had a celebration for the end of the problem.

* * * *

Chapter - 22

"He is a thief" Aditi shouted holding the sleeves of a sales man in the stores.

"Aditi, he has been working in the stores for five years. I know him well. He can't do that." Raghav said

"I have caught him red handed today. He was taking away cash from the cash box." Aditi said as she was still holding the man's sleeves. The man was giving a fearful expression as if Aditi was going to thrash her at any moment of time.

"I am sorry sir" the man pleaded for mercy

"Did you steal money from the cash box?" Raghav questioned the man without caring for the sorry.

"Yes sir I tried to take some cash but I will never do it again" the man said as he knew Raghav's rage.

"You will never ever get a chance to do it again" Raghav said and bang went his strong hands to knock the man down on the ground. Raghav kept on thrashing him till most parts of his body didn't start bleeding. It took Mayank, Rohan and me a long time to separate him from the man. Mayank soon fired the man out of the job before Raghav could kill him. Aditi and all of us hated thieves, as we always supported the truth.

Aditi was a single girl child to two of the well established IAS officers. Her mom and dad were placed in some rural district of Gujrat. She didn't want to stay with them. Or maybe she didn't want to stay away from Odisha. Her parents visited her very rarely due to a pressurized work schedule. And she had become an independent girl now.

They sent her a good amount for her expenditure. But she had also taken up a job in Raghav's store to manage her over expenditures. Sometimes the quality of our alcohol and cigarette hit our back hard. But we never compromised on the quality. I would at least never compromise on my Jonny Walker Black Label If I didn't have to follow Salu's restrictions. Some she had to earn the money for our useless activities. She shared the rooms with Neel and Sweety. She worked hard to earn just fourteen thousand bucks a month. She took all the pain talking to the customers throughout the night, and then managed her studies and college during the day. She had become stubborn after the tough way of life style. Now she had caught hold of a thief in the stores so she was taking out all the frustration of the day.

"Hey Aditi just relax and have some water!", Mayank said

"I am relaxed. Please get me some beer" she said and Raghav sent a worker in the store to fetch some beer for all of us. It was a party in the store. The lights were switched off and the shutter was down. Everyone had a bottle in their hands apart from me. I took my cell phone out and looked at Salu's picture. It seemed her photo even told me not to have a drink. I managed with some soft drinks. Now I didn't repent at all for not having a drink with my friends. I was happy with the soft drinks.

"Hey Guys can't we buy few more stores for a better profit" Mayank said as he always had plans of business expansion.

"But who is going to manage them and most importantly who is going to pay the heavy amount for the stores. I don't have a pie in my pocket." Raghav said with distress.

"I am going to be the buyer and let Aditi and Sweety manage them. They are doing so well" Mayank said and I was sometimes truly bored with Mayank's business man type conversations.

"Okay I agree but girls also need to agree" Raghav said and Mayank looked at the girls for their confirmation without speaking a single word.

"Okay but it's going to be very stressful" Aditi said looking at Sweety.

"That's done. Tomorrow we are going to buy three more stores in the new mall that has been made." Mayank said without caring to lend his ear to anyone. He usually has a habit of taking immediate decisions. But this time he was inculcating upon Sweety's habit of ordering without any one's consent.

"Your salary is doubled from this month" he continued before he could take the last sip from his bottle of beer.

"But…" Sweety tried to speak but Mayank injected her

"No queries. Can I have one more bottle please?" he shouted as the workers in the stores had become our waiters by now.

The next day the deal was finalized and Mayank was now the owner of three more stores. I am sure he is going to be as rich as the kings of Rajasthan as per his dreams if he went at this speed. I was very happy with all his success. I wanted him to rise at a greater pace than this. I would love to see him at great heights.

* * * *

Chapter - 23

My phone rang. It had disturbed me. I switched on my bed lamp and looked at my watch. It showed 3.00 am. Then my eyes went on to see my cell phone. It flashed "Salu calling". I was in a vile. I just hoped that there was no problem going on there.

"Hello my sweet Prince", Salu said with a joyful voice as I picked up the call.

"Hello", I said with a sleepy voice

"Were you sleeping? Did I disturb you?" She asked as an innocent kid.

"No I was just playing cricket with Brett Lee", I said trying to tease her.

"Shut up Mr. Gyan", she said as my purpose of teasing her was fulfilled.

"Okay I will put up my shirt but only after our marriage", I said continuing the process of teasing her. Telephonic conversations have a benefit of changing the phonetics of the actual words.

"Please Prince, stop it, I have good news for you", she said and I was very eager to hear the good news. Good news at this time is always of different types. I never had any idea what her good news was, that too disturbing my sweet sleep. I just hoped that the good news was more beloved than my peaceful siesta.

"What good news do you have at this hour of the day, maam?" I asked with a display of reluctance although I was very eager to listen to the news as soon as possible.

"You are going to fall down if I tell it to you", she said beating around the bush which I badly hated.

"Please will you come to the point, I am terribly sleepy", I said again trying to pageant my loath.

"Okay, the good news is…" she said elongating the last word which actually frustrated me this time as I interrupted.

"Are you going to complete your sentence this year dear, or do you need few more years to complete it" I asked with a very frustrating voice.

I wanted to hear the good news as soon as possible but she enjoyed irritating me as usual. This was her common habit of getting on to my nerves.

"Yes, I will complete it but only when I am in front of you next month" She said as I didn't get a single word from her statement. Or I thought maybe I heard something wrong.

"Did you tell that you are going to be with me the next month?" I asked just to re-confirm that the words which went into my ear before few minutes were not wrong.

"Yes, Minti di and I are coming to Odisha next month, without mom and dad, for attending a cousin's reception who got married to a person settled in Odisha. Mom and Dad have to go to meet Granny. She is having serious health hazards now a days" She said as I jumped off my bed. I was speechless. I could not believe my ears. Can something like this ever happen to me? It was a dream come true. One night I had dreamt of roaming with Salu on my bike in Bhubaneswar to which she had a hearty laugh. Now my dream was going to become a reality.

"Thank you so much for this splendid news", I said as I did not have anything else to tell her.

"It's okay now. Don't get over excited. You can sleep. Good night" She said and hung up. But it was absolutely impossible to sleep after such stunning news. I thought and made plans for what to do all over the night. I forwarded the text to my group members about Minti and Salu's arrival in Odisha next month. I did not get any reply. Probably it was a good night for everyone and they were enjoying their sleep. But it was the best night for me. I had gone mad. I kept on dancing with the music system with full volume the whole night. I knew I was disturbing my neighbours but I didn't care a damn about it.

The next morning I received the first call from Mayank. I expected his call to be the first as I had mentioned Minti's name in the text message. Even though he was in love with Reshma now he didn't miss a chance flirting with Minti.

"Hello sir, is your message a true one or are you trying to spread rumors" Mayank said without letting me even tell him good morning. He sounded more excited than me. His voice had become like a kindergarten kid enquiring about his favorite chocolate in a crowded shop.

"Yes dear it's true", I said confirming his queries

“Ohh yes”, He said extending the last word and repeating it again and again. He then hung up without even telling a bye to me. His reactions were most of the times out of my understanding level.

I received calls from all the members of our group confirming my message. Rohan’s first question was if I was drunk last night or was it true. I was the happiest person confirming everyone that it was absolutely true that Salu was going to come and it was not-at-all a rumour.

The whole month was the happiest month for me in the year. The wait seemed to be extending as each day seemed liked a year to me now. My heart beats were running with a very great pace as the days were coming closer. I had made plans for each and every hour she was here. My plans seemed to have been very hectic ones. But I had no fault of mine, she was just coming for five days and I had a plan of showing her the whole state which was absolutely impossible. It was a very short visit but the most important thing was that, it was a visit. I must have thanked her cousin’s fiancée a billion times for settling in Odisha, throughout the whole month.

* * * *

Chapter - 24

"Please dear, just listen to me" I said

"No Gyan I am not going to talk to him until and unless he stops getting involved in those fights", Reshma said and her face looked really furious. Mayank and Raghav had smashed down two cops on the road for taking bribe. Reshma and Mayank had not been couples till now, but Reshma had started taking care of Mayank more than any one of us. Both of them liked each other but I don't know why the idiot (Mayank) didn't ever propose to her.

"Okay I will talk to him. Now just chill" I said. We all were having a coffee at café coffee day, one of our regular places of chat. Mayank didn't dare to speak in front of Reshma's fury. He was not afraid of anything but always behaved like a mouse especially during Reshma's indignation.

"He is not going to change. He has become a lion who has tasted the human blood" She said and I didn't infer anything from her statement. I was sure Mayank was not a cannibal!! As much I knew him, he preferred vegetarian foods over non vegetarian ones.

Mayank got up from his seat pushing aside his coffee mug. He walked to Reshma with furious eyes. I just hoped that he didn't slap Reshma for calling him a cannibal. His walk and eyes increased my apprehension. I tried to stop him but he pushed my hands aside. He stood in front of Reshma's seat. Reshma left her place. Bugbear struck my heart. I crossed my fingers.

Suddenly I found something strange. I found Mayank, the stud kneeling down in front of Reshma and holding his ears with his face parallel to the ground. I could not believe my eyes. Neel was sitting beside me. I asked her to pinch me to confirm that I was not viewing a dream.

"I am sorry dear. This is not going to happen again." Mayank spoke with an innocent voice staying strong in the same position. I could see all the people in the café starring at him but he didn't care. This is what love does to a man.

Reshma was a peace loving girl who hated violence. She was in the same condition as me. She was the daughter of two working parents. Her dad was a successful business man and her mom worked for some social organization. So from the early age she had learnt how to live life independently. She cooked for herself when her parents were out. She took care of herself. She decided to have a boyfriend, who cheated on her and Mayank had smashed the guy down in the disco. Since then she became a member of our group. She was a good support to Mayank. She even sometimes advised him in his business plans. She was a very jolly type girl. So it felt good to have her in the group.

"Okay I can forgive you this time but a condition is applicable", she said and I felt she always had a condition for getting a job done.

"What condition do you have now? Do I have to smash down someone like your ex-boy friend?" Mayank asked in a low tone.

"No!! You are going to help me out in my physics practical", she said taking the advantage of the situation. Mayank got up from his kneeled down position in a surprise.

"What? I am not a good student. Raghav can help you out in your physics practical." Mayank spoke innocently looking at Raghav's face for help. Raghav was smart enough to turn his face and look at some hot chicks inside the café.

"No, I want you to write all my physics practical notes" she said and it was a very strong order.

"Okay" Mayank spoke like a wet cat and I could only smile at the situation.

* * * *

Chapter - 25

DAY 1 - 26th of August, 2010

It was the last week of August and the day finally came when my sweetheart was going to set her feet on the soil of Bhubaneswar. We were all desperately waiting for the train to arrive. I was the most desperate one. All the members of my group were there to welcome both the princess of Rajasthan. I was exceedingly nervous. My heart was pumping blood so hard that I was afraid that it would come out of my body. The train touched the platform at 10.40 am. As the train reached the platform Neel pulled me outside the platform. She took me to the car. She asked me to wait there until and unless they were not back with the two beauty queens. She actually was planning to shock Salu by informing her that I was not able to come to receive them, and then surprise her near the car. I followed her instructions as a puppet.

I waited desperately in the car to have a glance at my sweetheart. As soon as they approached the car I could see Salu's face. It seemed she was awfully upset with the news of my non-arrival. But as I moved out of the car and her eyes fell on me. She ran straight to me without caring about the world and hugged me tight. I could feel the amount of happiness she had on meeting me. I could feel the extent she loved me. The people around started starring at both of us as if there was some shoot for the bollywood movie going on.

"Hey my angel, my love, my princess" I said trying to bring her back to her normal state

"I love you" she said touching my heart.

"Love you too, my sweetheart" I said as I was hinted at by Raghav with his sign language to take our seats in the car. He didn't speak may be because he didn't want to waste my moment of love. No one spoke. Then I said hello to Minti hugging her in a casually warm way.

We moved on in our cars. It seemed to be a grand welcome arranged by Rohan and Mayank. They were actually good event managers. Three cars moving one after the other looked princely. Salu, Minti and me went on the black Scorpio. I drove the car as the rest followed us in the other cars. I had booked a four star hotel for their stay. It took us half an hour to reach the hotel Swosti Plaza. We had a short chat on reaching the hotel and then we left as to let them freshen up. We decided to meet in the evening for dinner and plan for the rest of the days. Although I had explained the entire plan to Salu over the phone but it was better to discuss them face to face to get better clarity.

It was 6.00 pm. I was the first to reach the hotel. It was quiet obvious. I asked the receptionist to inform Salu about my arrival. As soon as she got the information she ran to the reception and took me to their room. I was so excited but I had to share the space with her so called beloved di, Minti. I was hoping Mayank was there so that he could take away Minti from there.

"Hey buddy, come soon and take my headache away", I messaged Mayank as the reply came soon.

"Which headache dude", Mayank messaged

"Minti, your sweetheart", I replied

"Don't worry, Take care of my sweet heart, I will be there in next twenty minutes". He messaged.

Mayank reached the room number 302 exactly in twenty minutes. I was surprised.

"Were you waiting for my message to come here!!!!", I asked him in a very soft voice with a surprise on his arrival.

"Yes, I was beating up a pickpocket in front of the hotel when I received your message", he spoke softly to avoid any one around hearing him.

"Why do you always do that man?", I asked with frustration, as he always had to fight with someone or the other for some stupid reasons.

"Shut up and let me concentrate", He said with a very flirty voice. I thought he was trying to get into the mood of flirting so that he could have a good flirt with Minti. He always wanted to concentrate on girls who already had boyfriends. In the past whenever we discussed about the matter, Baba Mayank Dev's only reply would be *"there is no fun to sit on a chair where no one is sitting, but it's always adventurous to throw away a person from his seat and sit on the same chair."* Probably, he defined the chair as the girl and the person sitting on it as the girl's boyfriend. I never understood his idea of running after girls who were already committed to someone. He had more than a hundred failures in past with this stupid thought of his. And most importantly he had Reshma who loved him more than anything with him, even though the formal proposal session was not yet over.

We were discussing this when Minti and Salu entered the room.

"Hey Minti, Lets go for a drive", Mayank asked. I knew it well that if Reshma came to know about this she was going to stand on my neck before she could kill Mayank.

"Okay sure, why not?" She said and my heart started dancing.

"Then get ready, let's leave now" Mayank insisted

"Okay, then Salu you should get ready." She said looking at Salu and I started hating her at the same moment.

"No, I said only both of us. Let the lovers be together here", Mayank tried his best to convince. Although he had his personal benefits but I wanted to hug him at that moment. He was doing it for me in disguise.

"Okay then, but we should be back within an hour's time", She said as if the law of an hour had to be passed in the parliament.

"Yes dear, we will be back in the room sharp in one hour", Mayank confirmed her query

They left the room leaving both of us alone. I had asked Mayank to extend the timing from one hour to two. He asked me not to worry; he would somehow manage it. I knew once Mayank had told something it was done. I stopped worrying about them and started concentrating on my sweetheart.

We were lying down on the bed. Salu was looking extremely pretty with her blue eyes and her as usual pink lips which as usual forced me to kiss them. I didn't want to lose any chance of loving my sweetheart. This time it was a more passionate kiss than the last one. I loved it and am sure even she enjoyed it too. Our bond had become stronger now due to the passage of time. My head rested on the pillow and hers on my extended left arm. Both of us were overwhelmed. Love was in the air.

We had almost spent one and half an hour before the calling bell disturbed us. I got up from the bed and moved towards the door to find who the disturbing element was. I opened the door, it was Neel. I wanted to curse her for pestering our best moments. But it was dinner time and I had invited everyone for it. Slowly everyone arrived including Minti and Mayank. We moved down to the restaurant. It was a splendid dinner at last and most importantly a glorious day for me. Finally the day came to an end and we had to bid good bye.

* * * *

Chapter - 26

DAY 2 - 27th of August, 2010

I had exactly set the alarm clock at 5.30 am. We had planned a visit to Jagganath Puri, one of the famous four holy places in India. Our group had visited this place together more than a hundred times. We visited the place just to enjoy on the beach. I personally had visited Puri a hundred more times with my family. Everyone was well acquainted with the place. I wanted to take the blessings of Lord Jagganath with Salu.

Everyone was ready. We were at the gates of the hotel at 6.30 am. I had called Salu to ensure whether she was awake. I found out that she was ready and had been waiting for us since 5.30 am. She was really a punctual sweetheart of mine. The place was not of much interest to me but the interest of her being with me was the most. We had decided to take only the black Scorpio of Mayank so that there were no parking problems in Puri. Reshma was going to accompany us. She was going to meet Salu for the first time. They were very happy meeting each other.

We had planned the visit to the temple and the beach. Both the sisters never had the view of a sea before. It was common among the north Indians. One out of every hundred person would have seen a sea or ocean. It wasn't a long travel as the one from Jammu to Srinagar, but it took us almost two hours to reach the place. We had decided to visit the temple first and after taking the blessings of the Lord, we would visit the beach.

As soon as we reached Puri, we could feel heat. The crowded city itself gave the identification of the place. There were more priests than the general public. We had to take a long walk of about one and half kilo meters to reach the temple from the parking place. We reached the temple and completed all the procedures of security checking before the entry into the temple. As we were entering the main gate of the temple we could hear an old priest say some words.

"Heart is the only machine which works without any repair for years. So always keep it happy whether it's yours or others", he was speaking in the vernacular language. I heard it and turned to Salu giving her a smile.

She had not understood anything so I had to explain it to her. She reciprocated with a shy smile to me, when she completely got the meaning of the statement of the old priest.

We visited each and every temple in the huge campus containing a number of temples. It was a joyful experience for all of us taking the blessings of the deities. As we were moving out of the campus a priest stopped us to give us his blessings. He hit two sticks on our heads and said "May Lord Jagganath keeps both of you together forever." It was just unusually and unimaginably for me. I looked at Salu and smiled. I asked Salu to touch his feet with my expressions without speaking a single word. I even did the same. The priest gave me a flower to keep it with us. I divided the flower into two parts. One I kept in my pocket and the other I gave it to Salu to keep it with her. Then I had to explain what the priest said as he had spoken in the vernacular language. She just smiled and walked faster than her usual speed. I never understood her reaction. I can never forget these beautiful experiences with Salu.

We decided to take our lunch in some good restaurant to keep us away from starvation, before we could faint on the beach. We visited the Puri hotel to have our lunch. Every one ordered their favorite dishes. I even did the same for me and Salu. I was ordering Chicken tandoori for Salu but she stopped me.

"Hey, stop!!!" she said

"What happened? You love it." I said

"No, I am a vegetarian now" she said

"Why?" I was surprised. Instead I was absolutely shocked by her behavior.

"Just like that" she said

"But you loved to take non vegetarian food in Kashmir and you didn't even talk to me about this when I was with you in Rajasthan" I asked as I was very curious to know the reason for the sudden change in her food habits.

"She has even left touching non vegetarian food because you are a vegetarian", Minti said giving me the absolute correct statement for my question.

"But when did this happen? And why haven't you discussed anything with me about this till now?" I started to fire questions at her expecting the answers from her but I received the answers from Minti. Salu didn't even look into my eyes.

"The day we left Kashmir the very moment she decided that she would become a vegetarian" Minti clarified and I did not know how to react. Should I be angry with her for acting very childish? Should I be happy that she sacrificed something for me? Should I be sad that she had to leave out her favorite food for me? I did not know but I could not dare to order anything now. I asked her to order for both of us. And it was a perfect order for my taste. She knew it well what I liked.

- *Sweet corn soup with the slightest touch of butter*
- *Vegetable Biriyani*
- *Paneer Kofta*
- *Mushroom 65*
- *Baby corn sticks*
- *Mixed cabbage curry*
- *And finally the dessert was ice cream with hot chocolate sauce.*

The order she made for the food was unquestionable. Only my mom knew about my favourite dishes and ordered accordingly. But now my mom was going to have a competitor for herself. Salu had done the job of ordering so well that I was spellbound. I loved each and every dish she ordered starting from the starters till the dessert. I could not feel anything other than being a lucky man to get such a beautiful and understanding angel. I had already thanked God a billion times for giving her to me. I wanted to thank him a billion more times or even more.

It took us fifteen minutes to reach the beach from the restaurant. It was around 4.30 in the evening. The sun was planning to have a sleep. The wind was touching our skin making us feel good. We entered the beach, it was crowded as usual. Salu held my hand and walked forward. She didn't care for the crowd looking at us. I could overview some of the elderly person looking at us as if they had never seen a couple before with hands in hand. I even could hear an old man speak to a shopkeeper. He didn't have any idea that we were from the same state and knew the vernacular language. May be he thought we were tourists as we were conversing in Hindi and English because Salu and Minti were not well versed with our vernacular terms. I had taught Salu some words over our night conversations. She could understand some specific words but she could never speak them fluently.

"Today's youth has become absolutely shameless", he said

"Yes sir, every day I find many young people here with their girlfriends" the shopkeeper said with an excited voice as if he enjoyed looking at them. I looked at the old man's face. He seemed to be frustrated with the statement.

"Shameless creatures!!!!!!" he said giving an odd expression looking at our group. It struck Neel's ear drums. She looked at them. I knew something was going to happen.

"What do you mean by shameless creatures, uncle?" she fired her question at the old man. He was surprised with the vernacular language speaking girl. He entered into an absolute shock. The shopkeeper's mouth was wide open. It was wide enough for two large sized aquatic frogs to jump into it.

"I meant...", the old man started fumbling as he was interrupted by Neel.

"Better be very careful before you speak anything in front of the general public and especially when youngsters are in front of you" she warned as Rohan pulled her arms indicating her to stop. The old man was stunned at the statement. He did not have anything to speak.

We moved away from the place towards the sea. Minti and Salu were overwhelmed looking at the view. All of us were standing in a line enjoying the view of the sea when Salu pulled me away from the group. She held my hands tight and didn't let it go. Neither did she speak anything nor did she allow me to speak a single word. After a few moments of silence she spoke.

"Ruthkar apse hum kahan jayenge,

Yaad kiye bine hum kaise reh payenge.

Aapki haar muskan khushi he hamari,

Wada ki jiye aap humeshe kabhi dur na jayenge."

I did not have word to speak. I could only smile back at her. It was just perfect for the situation.

"Prince, please never leave me alone", she spoke

"How is it possible dear? I am incomplete without you." I said as I could see tear drops rolling down her cheeks. I could never tolerate her tears. It was difficult to control her tears. They were the tears of joy. The happiness of being with me was moving out of her beautiful innocent eyes. I didn't want to obstruct them.

We sat down on the sand away from the group. She spoke some important aspects of her life. For the first time she shared her career prospects of life. She wanted to be a crime reporter. She wanted to expose all the criminal politicians in front of the general public. It sounded a bit unconventional. She was a delicate darling of mine and these high sounding of-the-wall words from her had drowned me. But I liked it.

"Will you support me being a crime reporter, Prince?" She asked in her sugary filled innocent voice. It was obvious that her voice never suited the career option she had chosen.

"Yes, my dear Angel I will be the happiest person if you achieve your goal", I said in agreement

"Sure no", she asked again for a confirmation with her voice growing sweeter.

"Yes my sweetheart", I re confirmed my statement

"You will allow me to work after marriage no" She asked. I felt she had to take all the agreements from me on the beach, with some positive atmosphere all around.

"Yes my sweet honey", I said

"I love you my baby", she said and hugged me without caring for the people all around

"I love you too", I said as I could hear someone calling for me from behind. I turned to find out who it was? It was the disturbing element NEEL!!!! I wanted to kill her for disturbing my romantic moment for the second time in two days. She was showing me her wrist watch indicating that it was already late and we should leave now. I gave a hand signal that we were coming. Within a short time we had to leave the place. The next day the sisters had to attend the marriage party. On reaching early they would get some free time to rest before the hectic day of marriage of their cousin.

We reached the hotel within two hours and finally the day 2 had come to an end. Salu and I spent some special moments with each other today. We shared many important aspects of life. I loved each and every moment I spent with her. After I reached home my cell phone beeped with an incoming text message. It was Salu's message.

"Thank you for the lovely day Prince", she had sent

"*You are most welcome my angel*", I replied

"*I want something else from you*" she messaged

"*What?*" I replied with a surprise. I didn't have any hint of what she wanted.

"*I want to have a long ride with you on your bike at the late hours of the night*" she said and I was so happy to accept her offer.

"*Done; tomorrow after the marriage reception party I will take you for a long ride*", I replied

"*Thank you so much baby. Good night. Love you so much*", She replied

"*Love you too my Angel*", I replied and went to bed with her lone thoughts. The whole night went in sleeplessness. Her thoughts and words were revolving over my head till 5.00 in the morning. She had completely captured me now.

* * * *

Chapter - 27

DAY 3 - 28th of August, 2010

The vibration of my phone with the arrival of a text message opened my eyes. I looked into the screen to find out whose message had arrived early in the morning. I was traumatized when my eyes ran down my cell phone. I had 215 missed calls and 45 text messages!!!!! I turned to see my bed clock, it showed 12.00 noon. It was not early morning rather early afternoon. I had missed calls and received messages from Mayank, Raghav, Rohan, Neel, Sweety, Aditi, Minti and Salu. I knew I was going to be dead today. I forwarded a message to everyone to keep myself on the safe side.

"I am really sorry, could not get up this morning So, I was not able to receive your call" and forwarded to everyone.

I freshened up and got ready for a group scolding. I walked down the stairs and opened the gate to find out that there was the black Scorpio car parked in front of my house. I recognized it. It was our favourite car which belonged to Mayank. As soon as I went close to it, the door spontaneously opened from inside. The glasses of it were black so I could not find out what was the atmosphere inside. I entered the car with my fingers crossed. I was jolted. Everyone was inside it including Salu and Minti.

"You unabashed fool"

"You buffoon how dare you?"

"Your physics lecturer wasn't wrong when he called you a sleeping donkey", Neel said and my thoughts of the day got refreshed. My group could make any one feel guilty at any moment of time.

"What's the reason for your impudent behavior, stupid" voices struck my ear. I just spoke

"I am sorry guys, I was not able to get up early today, I am very sorry for my moronic behaviour", I said and smiled back at everyone. I could hear every one speaking something or the other in anger. But my sweetheart didn't speak a word. I wanted her to scold me or at least slap me. But there was no such reaction. When everyone had completed their share of hard words, Salu looked into my eyes. She didn't speak anything. Her eyes went numbed. She hugged me tight. It was very difficult for me to tolerate the situation. I started blaming myself. She had never scolded me before nor was going to do it in the future. She takes out everything on me with her tears. I would always prefer her scolding's to her tears. Her tears hurt me a lot more. But she had never been angry with me. She was surely the delicate darling of mine.

We went to some nearby places like the public parks and museums, to save time and get back to the hotel as soon as possible. So, both the sisters could get ready for the party. The whole day Salu did not speak much to me nor to anyone one else. She held my hand tight all throughout the day. She did not want to get separated from me. She was emotionally traumatized due to my irresponsible behaviour. I had done this with her for the second time today. I needed to be penalized but she did not do it.

After the day's visit we went to drop Salu and Minti in the hotel. As soon as Salu went out of the car she pulled my arm indicating to move out of the car. I stepped down to find out what it was.

"Do you remember your promise?" she asked.

"Yes, dear I remember it well", I answered with my guilt filled voice.

"So when are you coming to pick me up", She asked

"I will be there by 11.00 pm near the hotel" I said as the marriage party was to be held in the same hotel.

"I will be waiting for you sharp at 11.00 pm near the gate", she said

"Ok dear", I said and turned to take my seat in the car but she stopped me. She pulled my arm to turn me towards her. She came close to me and hugged me to throw away all the guilt which was still lying inside me. She had felt it in the short conversation we had.

"I love you Prince", she said

"I could never get someone as good as you", I said

"Don't worry I am only a single piece in the world" she spoke sarcastically to charge me up. She was utterly successful. All my guilty feelings were thrown a mile away from me by her. We left the place letting both the sisters to get ready for the party. As I knew it well that girls were going to take a long time to get ready.

I sat in my room relaxing and moving my eyes down at the messages I had received during the morning, when I was in the dreamland of my sleep. I could just look at it and laugh now. All the types of slangs in the world were used to text me by all my friends. May be they sat down together with a dictionary to find out the words to text me. I was looking at the clock on the wall. I was waiting it to strike 10.30, so that I could move out of the house. Each minute seemed to be an hour as time for the ride was coming closer. I wanted the clock to run faster and reach 10.30 pm. But the wait also had a different kind of amazing feeling. I wanted to make the night a special one for her.

Finally the wait was over and I started to reach the hotel in correct time. I was so excited to meet her that instead of 11.00 pm I reached the place at 10.00 pm. I had actually mistaken the clock. Instead of leaving the house at 10.30 pm I had left at 9.30 pm. I could only find out my mistake when I had reached the hotel. I had to wait for one more hour. And those became the longest period of my life.

But as soon as the clock struck 11.00 pm I could see a hot and beautiful girl coming out. The first expression which came out of my mouth was **wow!** When she came closer to me I found that she was Salu. She was wearing a blue translucent saree with her blue coloured backless blouse which was visible to some extent. Her light pink coloured lipstick made her look more gorgeous. It gave a contrasting effect with her blue eyes. Her long hair was falling down till her waist. She walked towards me with her high heels. She looked the prettiest ever girl I had seen in my life. I could see some youngsters as well as some old men looking at her with their widely opened eyes. When she came closer to me I was speechless. She kissed me and sat on the back seat. I had never thought of going on a ride with such a beautiful girl. I tried talking to her but she interrupted my statements.

"Just keep quiet and ride the bike as fast as you can. I want to make it the best night of my life", she said and hugged me tight from behind. We had a ride of nonstop one hour without a single word spoken by both of us. I could feel the warmth of her body. The roads were having very few people around as it was already midnight. We had already covered a distance of 80 kilo meters away from the city. I tried applying sudden brakes and each time I did that her grip on me became stronger. She came closer to me. It was virtually the most romantic evening of my life. I was riding with a great speed when suddenly she brought me to a halt.

"Stop the bike Prince" she said to nip in the bud of the ride. She got down from the bike. I could still feel the warmth of her body on my back. The first thought which struck my brain was that she had dropped something on the road and wanted to search for it.

"What? Did you drop something?" I asked with incredulity

"No, I want both of us to count stars" she said with her as usual innocent smile.

"What!!!!" I asked to ensure whether it was indubitably a bolt from the blue.

"Yes, I said I want to count stars" she said confirming that my ears had the correct reception.

"Have you gone crazy?" I asked with an agitated spirit.

"Yes honey I have gone crazy and please get down from the bike", she said using her innocent voice and her smile as a weapon to get on me. I had no other option other than getting down from the bike.

"Let's go there", she said pointing at a rock which was at a distance of thirty meters from us. The rock was big enough to easily accommodate both of us. She held my hand covering the distance between the bike and the rock. I never understood how she got such crazy thoughts at such point of times. She asked me to lay down on the rock. She herself lay down on the rock. Both of us were lying down with our eyes facing the beautiful looking sky and our feet hanging down the rock. She gave me a mark of the star from which I had to start my count. She took her own mark of the star from where she had to start her count. After ten minutes she asked me to stop my counting and demanded for the result.

"I have 353 stars", I said proudly as if I had bought them for myself

"I have 421 stars. Yipee I won!!!!!" she said with a very jolly voice. I loved her reaction. I enjoyed it whole heartedly.

Suddenly silence prevailed. She took my hand and kept it on her heart. I was out of idea of what she was trying to do. She turned her face towards me and asked

"What do you feel baby?" she asked

"Your heart beat and your love for me", I said proudly as I knew I owned her completely now.

"I will not be able to live a moment without you", she said as I could find her eyes shrinking.

"I will never let you live without me my angel" I said and took her into my arms to relax her. She could not control her tears and burst out. I did not speak a single word instead kept her tight in my arms to make her feel that I only belong to you. No one else has any right on me. After a few fervent moments we rode back to the hotel.

As we were riding back to the hotel, rats started running in my stomach. It was difficult to control them.

"I am very hungry. Let's reach the hotel soon and order something", I said as I was still riding the bike.

"Do you have any 24*7 shopping centre here?", she asked

"Why do you need a shop now?" I asked without caring to answer her question.

"I need two minute noodles to prepare for you", she answered

"But how are you going to prepare it without a Gas cylinder", I kept on firing the questions.

"Please get me the packet", she said and this time she did not care to answer my queries. And the orders of my delicate darling had to be followed. We went to a 24*7 shopping centre and purchased a two minute noodle packet. I could not see any other customers in the stall other than Salu and me. The clock had struck 2.00 am and usually people use the time to sleep unlike us; going for a ride, counting stars and purchasing two minute noodles.

We reached the hotel around 2.30 am. Salu took the keys of the room from the reception and both of us climbed up the stairs. Salu didn't believe in using the lift. Minti was still busy with the marriage rituals. So the room could be occupied by only both of us. She opened the door and we entered.

"How are you going to prepare this now?" I asked as I was very excited to know what she was going to do with the noodles. Or did she want me to eat them raw!! She did not bother to reply. She started opening her bag and searching for something. After a few minutes of intensive search she took out a mini coffee heater from her bag.

"Please ask the waiter to bring in a plate and a fork", she spoke after a long gap of silence and I followed her orders. The plate and the fork were in the room within ten minutes.

She had already started doing her work. She took the designer bowl placed on show case of the room and poured water into it. She started heating it with the coffee heater. It seemed crazy but her passion seemed beautiful. After heating the water she put the two minute noodles into it with all its ingredients. It took a bit more than two minutes but finally it was prepared. She served them on the plate brought by the waiter. She came close to me and sat next to me with the plate. By this time rats in my stomach had eaten up half of my stomach. She feed me. With a single bite of the noodle from her hand, the rats vanished. She kept the plate aside and hugged me tight. This time she was doing the job of consoling which was usually my part. The noodles seemed better than normal made over the gas cylinder. May be because she had made it or had fed me with her hand, but it tasted outstanding.

After dinner, we lay down on the bed adjacent to each other. I put my hand on her waist and her eyes closed down spontaneously. We came close to each other. She opened her eyes looking into mine with deep intensity. I pulled her close to me. The air was full of romance. Her blue eyes had captured me completely. Our lips came in contact with each other. I could get the taste of her lip stick. I had almost taken of all her lip stick with my lips. Slowly my lips moved down her neck to put her into the galvanization of romance. My hands moved from her waist to her bosoms passionately. She moved her hand and the upper part of the saree moved away from her body. My lips moved down opening half the blue colored backless blouse. My hands slowly went inside her blouse. This had ignited both of us. My lips then moved to her stomach to kiss it. I gave her a love bite on the stomach. She made a bit of noise but we both enjoyed it. She removed my shirt. I removed her blouse completely. My hands engaged themselves playing with her boobs. Our lips engaged kissing each other wildly.

After a few moments something struck my mind. I had promised her something when we were together for the first time in Kashmir. I had promised her that I will never let her down in front of society. I knew she would not stop me from doing anything as she had completely surrendered herself to me and most importantly she trusted me. I stopped everything at that point of time and hugged her hard. Tears rolled down. But this time from four eyes than two eyes. We had surrendered ourselves to each other.

"I will not let anything separating both of us", I said promising her with tears still rolling over my cheeks.

"I can't let you go anywhere dear", she said and burst out with a heavy flow of tears.

"Don't worry angel give me some time then I am going to bring you here forever", I said

"I am waiting for my Prince" she said as she still lay in my arms. It took us some time to get normal. It was now next to impossible for any obstruction to separate us. We were still on the bed when she asked.

"Do you like kids?"

"Yes, I do. But why are you asking this?" I asked

"I want to visit an orphanage with you and spend some time with kids there" she said to my astonishment.

"Okay, but how do these ideas come to you", I asked as I was very impressed with her wish. Even I had seen her helping nature at the Jammu railway station, when she had helped the old blind man.

"I always had a wish to visit an orphanage and help the kids after getting you in my life" she spoke as my old granny now to which I had a hearty laugh.

"Okay my sweetheart we will visit an orphanage tomorrow at 11.00 am, wait for me", I said promising to fulfil her wish and got up from the bed to leave.

It was time for my departure. The clock had already struck 5.00 am. The sun was coming out slowly. It had been the best night we had spent together. Nothing can be better than this one without my Salu. I wanted to stay with her forever. I didn't know when the time and society would allow us to be together forever. Our souls were one now.

* * * *

Chapter - 28

DAY 4 - 29th of August, 2010

"I am going to enjoy today" Salu said as we were moving towards the orphanage. It was around twenty five kilometres away from the city. She had a different kind of glee in her eyes. All the group members were accompanying us, but with a bent neck. They were not enjoying the visit. Sweety and Raghav didn't even care to visit the orphanage. There were only two persons who were happy. They were Salu and me. I did not have much interest in the orphanage visit, I was happy because Salu was happy.

"When did the ghost of social work jump into your head" Minti asked looking at Salu. She was not very curious either visiting the orphanage.

"The time I got my sweetheart in my life", she responded without any hesitation.

We stopped on the way to purchase some eatables for the children of the orphanage, as instructed by Salu. She bought cakes, biscuits, pizzas, burgers and toys for the kids. It felt good for the first time doing something positive for others. It took us another forty minutes reaching the orphanage after shopping.

As we entered the orphanage I felt something. Salu held my hand as we were entering the gate. My soul seemed to become happy while I was entering. I felt purified. We went to the manager and asked his permission for meeting the children. He was a very kind hearted and generous personality. He looked old enough to be called as grand pa. I could even see children around me who came to him with their queries and problems calling him grandfather. He had very less hair on his head with brown eyes. He had a good personality. Most importantly he assembled all the kids around to make it easy for us to meet them.

Salu distributed all the stuffs she had bought for the kids. There were kids of age three months till fourteen years old kids. As per the manager after the age of fourteen they send the kids to a different place where there were more qualified, well trained and educated people to take care of them.

While I was talking to the manager in a distance I could see Salu playing with the kids, feeding them and talking to them in a motherly way. It was absolutely a beautiful sight at least for my eyes. I could see the love for the kids in her eyes. She was carrying the three months old kid in her arms and kissing him as a mother does to the newly born baby. My mere words cannot describe the happiness that glowed out of her face playing and feeding the kids with her own hand. The respect I had for her increased to an enormous height that very day. She was really an angel sent down by God for me.

Mayank, Neel, Rohan, Minti and Aditi were also enjoying playing with satisfaction. I had never seen any of them happier than they were the same day. I had only seen Mayank happy when he thrashed down someone. But he seemed happier today. I didn't know that my decision of bringing all of them was correct or not. But after seeing their spirit in the orphanage I thought that it was a colossal decision to bring all of them together. After spending three hours in the orphanage we were planning to leave. The manager requested us to have our lunch with them. They had prepared some delicious food for us on our arrival. We had our lunch with some of the trustees and the manager. As we were walking out of the gate, the manager called us from behind.

"Daughter, the job which you have done today was the first time I have seen in my thirty five years career", He said putting his both hands over Salu's head. To which she bent down touching his feet taking his blessings.

"Sir, I promise every time I come to Odisha I would spend a day with these kids", She said and her voice seemed to be much mature this time. It was never the same innocent one I knew.

"May God bless you and all your friends and you remain happy forever", the manager said.

"My happiness lies with this man sir. If he is happy I am also happy", She said pointing to me and turned to hold my hand with the same amount of love she had for the kids. We bade goodbye to the kids and the manager and sat inside the car. There was a contrastive silence inside the car. I could never expect my group to be so hushed. And in the past I had never seen them in such tranquility. Everyone had a mature smile on their faces.

"Guys let's have a cup of coffee in Café coffee day" Minti spoke breaking the silence

"Okay, that's a good idea" Mayank said and moved the car towards the desired destination.

We caught hold of our favorite table in Café coffee day. The manager recognized us as we were regular customers to the café. I had called Sweety and Raghav to join us there. They were on their way. The most astonishing thing was the noiselessness which prevailed in the presence of my group.

"Is someone going to talk?" I asked breaking the subdue.

"Salini, you have given us the most precious moments of our life" Neel spoke to my startle. Although I didn't get anything, for the first time in my life I heard Neel speaking in such a serious tone.

"What do you mean dear?" I asked softening my tone

"Yes Gyan, both of you have given us the ultimate happiness taking us to the orphanage" Mayank spoke with a very serious voice with his favorite sizzling brownie in his hand. I was nauseated. Mayank and the word serious could never sail on the same boat. But I found Mayank speaking seriously which took me to the state of perturbation. It was like Sachin Tendulkar talking about ice hockey.

"Have you all gone mad?" I asked trying to chill the atmosphere. As I completed my statement Neel got up from her seat pushing aside her coffee mug. She went straight to Salu and held her hand. I was amazed at what was going on there. Salu got up from her seat.

"Thank you my sweet little sister" Neel said and hugged her tight. I could see tears in her eyes. I had never seen Neel shed tears before even when she had left her dad's place. This visit to the orphanage had actually touched her.

"Hey, stop it I am jealous now", I said exerting myself to relax the atmosphere.

"Shut up idiot and come here", she said as I left my place and went close to her. She hugged Salu and me together with both her hands and all had a hearty laugh.

"I love both of you", she said with a smile still hugging us. It was cool now; the serious atmosphere was not prevailing any more. Sweety and Raghav had entered the café. Moreover I could have my coffee peacefully now.

We reached the hotel, it was already evening. We had a bit of group chat before Minti ordered for the food in the room. Finally the beautiful day had come to an end. We had to leave. As soon as I reached home I received a call from Salu.

"Hey Prince, have you reached home?" Salu asked

"Yes, my sweetheart. Haven't you slept yet?" I asked

"No, your thoughts are not letting me sleep", she said

"WOW!!!!! So what am I doing with you in your thoughts? Am I teasing you?" I asked sarcastically

"Yes, you are teasing me. So I called you up to tell you to stop teasing me" She said flirting with me.

"Okay I will stop it, now go and sleep", I said

"I will but tomorrow is my last day so I want to see the sunrise with you here", she said

"Okay my dear anything for you. Get ready by 4.00 am. I will wait for you in front of the hotel gate." I said and hung up. I went to bed as I had to fulfill her desire of viewing the sunrise with me. I had never seen sunrise since my birth. It was going to be my best morning.

* * * *

DAY 5 – 30th of August, 2010

"You are always late", Salu said as I was late by thirty minutes and she had been waiting for me since 4.00 am.

"I am so sorry baby", I said in a childish voice with my motorbike's engine still on.

"Okay, now just stop buttering me and let's go. Where are we going?" she asked

"There is a beautiful temple here; we can have a perfect view of the sunrise", I answered her queries.

She held my hand as we reached the temple. The temple was on a small hill away from the city. The air was cool in the morning and it was very romantic to be with her in such an atmosphere. The sun slowly came up. It was outstandingly beautiful.

"Good morning Mr. Sun" I said kidding around to which she hit me on my right arm. She was folding her hand with closed eyes in front of the Sun God. She had put the dupatta on her head. I preferred to look at her than folding my hands. But I had to fold them on her insistence.

We walked around the beautiful temple hand in hand, till we reached a crystal clear pond. It was a temple property. We stood there for long till a priest came close to us.

“Son, throw a coin and ask for a wish and it is going to be true” he said and left the place.

“Stupid things, they take away money from people using these tricks” I said showing my disinterest in these activities.

“Give me two coins please”, Salu asked

“Have you gone crazy? Do you believe in all these things?”, I asked with a source of distress.

“Yes dear, you know it well that I am crazy. And you have fallen in love with a crazy girl” she said making fun out of me.

“Stop it. Let’s go to some peaceful place and have a chat”, I said ignoring her statements

“No first give me two coins”, she said and her voice had grown serious now.

“Are you serious?” I asked but she did not answer. She looked into my eyes. I understood I had to follow her instructions. I took out two coins from my wallet and handed it over to Salu. She kept one in her hand and pushed the other into my fist forcibly as I was a bit reluctant.

“Now close your eyes, put the coin into the pond and ask for your wish” She instructed and I followed her instructions. After performing the act she asked me

“What wish did you ask for?”

“I want to be a successful businessman”, I said very innocently

“What did you ask?” I continued

“Not now, I will tell you once I reach Rajasthan”, she said

“This is unfair”, I said with an eagerness to know what her wish was.

“Everything is fair in love and war. And my dear I have fallen in love with you” she said pressing my cheeks and started walking.

“Please tell me what you asked for?” I requested with a very innocent voice hoping that she would tell me. But all my efforts went into the pond where the coins had sunk.

We walked some distance and found a cool place to sit and have a chat with each other. We discussed our future plans. It was lovely to have a chat with your lover in the early morning on a hill top, that too in a pure place like a temple. Our chats elongated till we received a call from Minti to reach the hotel. We always had never ending talks. But we had to hurry before Mayank could stand on my neck till death. He had asked me to be near the hotel by 8.30 am and it was already 9.30 am. We rushed to the hotel.

We did not want to make the day very hectic for the girls as they had to catch the train in the evening. We decided to visit the nearby places and return to the hotel room by the afternoon so that they could have a proper lunch and rest before they could board their train. The day seemed very short. In fact the five days seemed very short to me. The amount of happiness and enjoyment we had in the past few days were the best moments of my life.

It was time for departure as the clock had already struck 6.30 in the evening. The train's arrival time was exactly at 8.00 pm. They checked out the hotel. It was a very painful separation. Both wanted to cry but had to stand strong to support each other's emotions. We reached the station at 7.30 pm. We still had half an hour in hand. I wanted the train to get cancelled or something like that to happen. I wanted to spend some more time with her. She held my hand and pulled me away from the group.

"What happened dear", I asked with a drowned voice. She took out a packet from her bag and handed it over to me. I opened to see what it contained. It had a blue shirt, a pair of black jeans and a photo album. I kept the shirt and jeans aside and eagerly opened the album. It contained photographs of Kashmir and Bhubaneswar visit designed in a collage. The album contained only our photos.

"Wow!!! How did you make it? And when did you make it?" I started firing questions in excitement

"Neel di helped me in designing this", she said and I handed over a packet to her which contained gifts for the Chittra family. I had gifted her pair of pure white jeans and a blue tops. She loved it.

Our conversation was still on when the train arrived. We arranged their luggage as per their assigned seat numbers. The train soon left taking my Salu away from me. She stretched her hands out of the window to bid me goodbye. I could not tolerate the separation. I wanted to keep her with me but the thoughts of the smug face of the idli sick bastard didn't allow me to do that. A drop ran down my eyes. Neel hugged me trying to support me. But the beautiful five days were gone for which I had waited for a month. I didn't know when these days will come back to my life. I badly wanted her with me soon. The happiness I received was too much for me to process at just one go. I reached home and opened the photo album. Tears ran down to touch the collage. My phone rang to distract me from my thoughts.

"Hey my Prince, please don't cry" Salu said from the other side of the phone in a very shaky voice, as if she had just stopped crying after a long crying session. I don't know how she came to know about my situation even though I did not speak a single word.

"When did you stop crying, dear" I asked trying to keep my voice jolly.

"Just now", she said with an artificial smile, may be to relax me.

"I want to come to you", I said without having a control over my emotions

"Yes, I am waiting for you Prince" She said and hung up. Tears ran down from her eyes. Although she did not want to let me know that she was crying but I still felt it.

The whole night I looked at the album and the gifts she had given me. I was missing her a lot now. She was going to reach on the 1st of September. I could have a good chat with her then. I had to wait till then. I knew each second was going to charge me heavily.

* * * *

Chapter - 29

I lost her forever..........

I received the first call from Salu on the 1st of September in the evening. I had been looking at my cell phone's screen again and again for her call or message since the morning. I was feeling restless. I had even tried calling her but the operator said that her number was out of the coverage area.

"Hello prince. How is my naughty boy?" she said elongating the word prince and my heart cooled down listening to her voice.

"Your naughty boy was dying to listen to your voice" I said,

"Is it?" she said stretching her words longer to tease me,

"Why didn't you call me earlier?" I fired my question,

"I have just reached home. I haven't even changed my clothes" she said,

"I have been madly waiting for your call" I said,

"ooo my baby… I am so sollllly" she said, twisting her words as usual to make me happy.

"Okay you are forgiven but you have to call me after you freshen up", I said,

"Yes sure my dear sweetheart" she said and hung up. And I started looking into the album which she had presented me. I smiled to myself. I was so happy with the precious gem of my life.

Both of us very happy and we had long chats at the late hours of night on the 1st and 2nd of September. On 2nd September we had a talk for almost for six long hours starting from 11.00pm to 5.00 in the morning. She told me she wanted to join a university in Odisha for her journalism so that she could spend some precious moments with me. I told her that I would give her the confirmation about the universities within two days. As we had talked for a long that night she decided to go for a morning walk without going to bed.

"I will call you as soon as I am back my Prince", she said

"Okay dear" I said

"But I need my kiss now" she said twisting her words

"No, you are going to get them only when you come back and give me a call" I said

"Please no, Prince" she requested

"NO", I stuck strong to my past statement,

"Okay sleep as much as you want to, but I need it once I come back", she said and hung up.

I slept and got up at 10.30 am. I searched for my cell phone. I looked into my screen but I could not find any miss calls from Salu. I was shocked. I called her up. For the first time no one picked up the call. I called her for the second time.

"Gyan" came the sobbing from the other side of the phone. It was not Salu.

"Who is this?" I asked

"I am Minti here" she said as she was still sobbing

"Why are you crying? What has happened?" I asked,

"Salu is no more with us" she said as I could not get her words at the first instance.

"What do you mean?" I asked and by now my heart had almost choked. I got up from my bed.

"She had gone for morning walk and a drunken man in a black Scorpio car ran over her. We are taking her body for cremation now." she said.

The phone fell out of my hand. My body felt weak. My mind stopped working. It went blank. Darkness fell in front of my eyes. I didn't know what to do at the point of time. I took the support of the wall to sit on the ground. I lay down on the ground unconscious. After regaining consciousness I called Mayank and asked him to come to my place at the moment. It didn't take him much time to understand that something was wrong. His arrival took a whole of six hundred seconds. I was sitting on the ground with both my hands on my face. Till now I could not believe Minti's statement. I felt Salu would call me up and tell that it was just a prank which she played on me taking Minti's help and she wanted all her kisses right now. But no such thing happened. I blamed myself for not stopping her from going for the morning walk. I never knew that it was going to be the last time I would be talking to my angel.

I told Mayank about it on his arrival. He helped me getting up from the ground. He gave me a glass of water to recover me from my trauma. Mayank called up everyone and informed them about the situation. I was not able to walk. He supported me taking me away from my room. He took me to his house. All were present there from before. Neel hugged me hard and cried aloud. But I don't know what happened, I could not speak a single word nor could I cry. May be I was expecting a call from Salu. I wanted to listen to her voice but she never called. I kept staring at my phone again and again but it didn't have any effect. Mayank wanted me to cry before I went into depression so he slapped me many times. But nothing worked I was not able to speak a single word.

Everyone stayed back with me till the evening. I tried to speak but the co ordination between my tongue and mind always failed. I tried to speak something but the word which came out of my mouth was "Salu". My mind had stopped thinking of anything other than her name. Mayank had called Minti in the evening. She had told him in details of what had happened. Mayank had never expressed anything in front of me. Finally I insisted Mayank to drop me back at home. He didn't want to leave me alone nor did anyone else want, but my insistence of spending some time alone forced them to fulfil my wish.

It was the worst day of my life. Three days back I had dropped her at the railway station and now she would never come back to me again. I sat down on my bed took out all her gifts and started staring at them. The watch she had gifted me had struck 12.00 in the midnight. It was time for her to call me. I flipped my cell phone, which had her picture saved as my wallpaper. But I realized that her call would never come again. She was no more. She was killed by a drunken driver. I tried telling all these things to myself but my heart never agreed to these true facts. My heart told me that she was going to call me now. A serious battle between my heart and mind was on. I picked up my phone and dialled her number. A ray of hope enlightened in my heart when her number started ringing.

"Hello Gyan" an upset voice came from the other side of the phone. It was Minti.

"Hey Minti why did she do this to us", I asked trying to control the beads running out of my eyes.

"I don't know Gyan. She is very bad" She spoke emotionally and then busted out. In fact Salu was her younger sister, and they were very close. I could feel her pain, but was there anyone to understand my pain.

"Don't worry dear. Everything will be all right", I said and hung up.

It's always difficult to keep track of the time when you are happy as it passes away so fast but at the same time the bad time never lives you alone. You can only think of the happy moments when you are crossing through such a phase of bad time. I went back to my thoughts. I looked into the album which she had presented me. Her photos looked so lively. I felt she would come out of the photo and kiss me. But they were all my illusion. A person who goes away from us never comes back. Can't the same days ever come back so that I could stop her from going for her morning walk? My heart said she will come back to you but my mind said a big "no". I never knew whom to trust. It was practical to accept the reality but my heart didn't allow me to do so.

I thought of the night when we had gone for a ride. I thought about the unsafe place where she wanted to count stars. I thought of the time we had spent all alone in the hotel rooms. I thought of the time when I slept on her lap and she moved her hand over my head. I thought of the heart shaped parathas that she had prepared for me. Will those days ever come back? These thoughts never allowed me to shut my eye lids even for a second.

The next day I went down early in the morning as I could never sleep for a minute. Mom was happy that after so many days I had left the bed early, but she didn't know about the pain I was going through. I had to behave normally with my family. I didn't want anyone to know about my emotional traumas. I walked straight to Mayank's house. He had not left his bed. Once he saw me he was surprised. He took me inside and prepared some breakfast for me. But I denied. I had not even taken a sip of water since I had heard the news. But amazingly I didn't feel hungry.

* * * *

Days passed and I started having a transition of attitude. I preferred to speak less and kept myself busy, racking my memory with Salu's thoughts. Sometimes you want to scream with pain, but at the same time something forces you to freeze. I was frozen at the moment. I had to romp my way through the difficult times without anyone holding my hand. I could never expect Mayank to handle me twenty four hours a day.

I could not tolerate the black Scorpio car that Mayank owned. Even other black Scorpio cars also became my utmost enemies. I felt it was the killer of my sweetheart. Mayank sold the car immediately at a very low price without caring for the loss he suffered. My friends were trying to make me as comfortable as they could. But no one could take Salu's place in my life. Almost a week had passed since Salu's death and I had been surviving only on water since then. Mayank, Reshma and Neel forced me to have something. This time Mayank was furious. He promised that he would not take a sip of water till I don't take food. I was forced to have my food. Mayank prepared some noodles and fed me. My mind went back to the night when Salu had prepared noodles for me with the help of coffee heater. I hugged him hard and cried aloud. It was the first time I had cried. No one stopped me. They wanted me to cry and throw away all the hard feelings away from my heart.

My mom had smelt something by now due to my changed attitude. After all she was my mother and mother's heart always beats with the child's. She asked me a hundred times about my changed reactions but I felt safe avoiding the topic. I was normal with the family. No one other than my mom could feel my stress. It was just like, a serious and disastrous crap had happened around me and I just smile and then decide to move away.

On the 11th of September I was laying down on the sofa flipping through a novel when the calling bell disturbed me. I went up to see who the person was. I opened the door to find out, it was the post man.

"Mr. Gyan", the post man said

"Yes, I am Gyan", I said clarifying his queries.

"There is a letter for you" he said and handed over the letter to me. I was surprised. There was no one who sent me a letter other than Salu. I opened it. It was an absolute shock to me. The name written on it was Salu. How was it possible? My sub conscious mind told me that she was back. I turned the letter to find out the date and it showed 3rd of September. It was the last letter from her that she posted before the car ran over her.

Salu's Last letter to me:

My Honey,

Firstly I want to thank you for everything. You have given me the most precious moments of my life. I want to live it again and again with you. Your eyes are rotating in my mind's periphery. I want to watch it forever.

It's really going to be difficult living without you now. And I am sure you are never going to let anything difficult happen in my life.

Prince, I remember the late night ride on the bike. I can still feel the warmth of your body and I want to feel it forever. I can still visualize the stars we counted together and I want to count them for the rest of my life. I can still smell the two minutes noodles we had in one plate. I can still feel your lips on mine when we were on the bed and I want to feel them again and again. I can still feel your hand touching all the parts of my body. As I am writing this letter I want to stop writing and run back to you and I am sure you are going to hug me tight. I want you to hug me with same intensity of love throughout my life.

Baby, do you remember the coin we dropped in the temple's pond? You had asked me about my wish but I had not disclosed it. I had asked God to keep us happily together forever. It was my wish. I would like to add another wish to it. I want you to be successful in life and take me away as soon as possible. This separation is very intolerable on my part now, baby. I want to hold your hand and roam around in each of the streets of Bhubaneswar.

My naughty boy, you never cry in front of any one. You try to prove very strong. But I know my sweetheart has a very soft and delicate heart. I promise you that I will never hurt my darling's heart. I need thousands of kisses from my naughty boy. And remember, I am not going to compromise on that. I love it when you call me with names like princess and angel. I am always going to be an angel in your life. I love you my darling and I will love you forever.

Shona, do you remember the orphanage. I am missing it badly. I am missing the three month's old kid. I am missing the games we played that evening with the kids. I loved to be with them. Please visit the orphanage at regular intervals. I will feel as if I am spending time with the kids. I also have a dream of having a kid who is going to be my doll. I want a son like you, a cute son, as loving as you. I have attached a cheque in the name of the orphanage with the letter. Please give it to the manager on behalf of both of us. And remember to call me as soon as you receive this letter.

Your sweet baby angel,
Salu

I turned the letter to find a cheque of rupees ten thousand attached to the letter. Tears fell from my eyes making the letter wet. I took the letter close to my heart and cried hard to throw out my emotions. I wanted to kiss her. I wanted to write a reply to the letter, but the person to whom I had to reply was no more with me. She had left me all alone in this world. I wanted to go for a ride in the late hours of night with her and do all the crazy things she wanted to do. I wanted to view the sunrise with her. I was ready to throw all the coins made in the country in the pond. I wanted to hold her hand and roam in each and every street of Bhubaneswar. But I knew it was not possible. I could only refresh my thoughts. I wanted to call her and tell that I received her letter and tell her how much I loved her as per the last line of her letter but……

I ran to Mayank's place with the letter and the cheque in my hand. I was in my shorts. I was so much into pain that I even forgot to wear my shoes. I knocked at the door. Mayank opened the door and gave a very shocking expression. I was in a very bad condition. He didn't ask me anything and hugged me hard. He took me in and made me comfortable on the sofa. I didn't want to leave him. I was shivering. I was just like a kid of five years then, who was missing his mother. Salu was more like a second mother to me. He held me hard trying to make me more comfortable. I could not speak anything and just handed over the letter and the cheque to him.

As soon as he completed reading the letter I could feel his tears on my skin. He hugged me hard and for the first time in my life I saw the stud, Mayank cry. He didn't want to live me alone nor did I want to stay alone now.

* * * *

I was a changed personality now. I had become more aggressive than Mayank and Raghav by now. I felt as if I had miserably failed in my life. I had given up faith in God. I kept cursing the Lord for what he had done to me. Every small thing frustrated me now. I started hating visiting places where I could over view couples. I took up fights with some of the dangerous criminals of the city. I moved around with a revolver and a bottle of alcohol every time. I was drunken 24×7. Although I had promised Salu not to drink but I could not manage my pain without it. I broke my promise made to her. I felt guilty but the felling of guilt was much less than the pain of my heart. Without alcohol sometimes I felt someone is making holes in my heart with a sharp needle. Time passed and my aggressive conduct increased. In other words I had become a hard core spoilt brat. I knew my Salu could never tolerate me in such a condition, but I needed to divert my thoughts before I could get into the mode of depression. Every evening I would spend at least two hours with the album in my hand all alone in my room and cry till my heart was satisfied.

After a month's time I went to the orphanage. The manager was very happy to see me. I had taken cakes, biscuits, pizzas, burgers and toys as Salu had done last time for the kids.

"How is Salu, Son?" the manager asked as soon as he came near me.

"Sir..." I paused for a moment

"What happened son, any problem?" he spoke

"Sir she is no more. A car ran her down just after three days she left Bhubaneswar" I said trying to control myself.

"What?" he said and I could feel his traumatized state. He sat down on the ground. I helped him getting up and some of the kids helped him with water.

"Why does God do things like this to good people" he said as I helped him sit on a chair.

"These are some food items and toys for the children and most importantly this is a cheque of ten thousand for the orphanage fund which Salu had sent" I said and the manager went to a source of consternation. He could not speak anything as I handed over the cheque to him. He put his left hand on his fore head and kept starring at the cheque.

"I will visit you regularly sir", I said and moved out.

I could see the three months old kid with an orphanage attendant. Salu had enjoyed a lot of time with the kid when she was here. The kid had grown a month older now. I went close to him and took him in my arms. I just kissed him and moved away.

I was moving outside the gate when a seven year old kid came running to me and pulled my shirt. I turned around to see who it was. I had seen him interacting with Salu when she was here.

"Bhaiya, where is Salu di? I am missing her a lot" He asked and I didn't have any answer. I bent down my knee to come in level with his face.

"She is also missing you a lot dear..." I said and moved my hand over his head. Then I walked out of the gate with tears in my eyes. "I am missing you baby. Why did you do this to me?" I said to myself looking up into the sky. I am sure she must have heard me wherever she was.

* * * *

Chapter - 30

Another Big Loss of My Life

Our entire group members had started working for a political party. Mayank, Rohan, Raghav and me had become the right hand of the party leaders, as we were very popular in the area. The girls also used to help us to some extent. Moreover I was able to recover from the pain of losing Salu, getting myself involved in the party work. I was in regular touch with Minti now. She had not yet recovered from the trauma of losing her sister. It was an unbreakable bond which was broken by the Lord. I could understand her pain but could not do much for her.

I tried to keep myself busy with studies and the party work. My frustration had yet not decreased. The anger was still growing in my inner soul. The party work was fuel to the fire in me. We needed much of muscle power and I was ready to use them all. I wanted to keep rest of my group away from this work but they didn't allow me all alone.

One day after some work of the party we were returning home. Suddenly there was an attack on us by the opposition. We were not ready for such a situation. Firing opened up between both the parties. Neel was the best shooter in our group. She was a gold medallist in shooting. In the past, I had fired some bullets blankly into the air but it was the first time I had to shoot at the persons in front of me.

We were just seven of us and our rivals were almost more than fifteen. Before I could start firing, Neel had already fired three people on their legs. They were down on the ground. Mayank looked at me and blinked before each round of bullet he fired, as if he was playing with an air gun. The rivals were now sort of bullets so they had decided to run away. I could see them flee away and we celebrated.

As we were celebrating instantaneously Mayank fell on the ground on his face. The road was filled with blood moving out from his neck. It didn't take us long to know that a bullet had struck him. I took him into my arms, putting one hand on his wound to stop the flow of blood. He held my hand tight.

"Gyan, please take care of yourself and Reshma", Mayank said suffering from a lot of pain.

"Hey don't worry buddy we are going to the hospital now. Everything will be absolutely fine", I said but he was not ready to listen to me. He stared at everyone.

"Bye... Everyone take care of yourselves. And you are the best family I have ever got in my life. I love you all." he said and closed his eyes. I kept pronouncing his name and shaking his body with a hope that he will get up, but that didn't happen. It was another big loss of my life before I could completely get out of my past pain. I didn't know the ways out to survive my life now.

We took his body to his place. Reshma was informed about the situation by Neel. None of us were in a condition to support each other. Reshma went close to Mayank's body. She moved her hand over his head and kissed his forehead. Raghav and I were covered in blood as we had carried the body inside the house. There were thousands of people waiting to see his body. Many ladies from the slum were crying badly because their saviour was no more to save them. Mayank was also a saviour in all of our life. We had lost an important part of our life.

I didn't have any idea of God's plans. Was one loss not enough for him in my life? Did he want to take few more gems from my life? I blamed myself and my selfishness for killing my friend. If I would not have joined the political party he would never have been dead.

Reshma came close to me and hugged me hard to control her tears but both of us could not stop our tears. I knew although they were not a couple but they loved each other more than a couple. I could understand her condition better than anyone else. She was facing the same situation which I faced a few days back. She hugged me and spoke

"I loved that idiot but he didn't even care to wait for me." She said and I didn't have words to console her.

We took the body for cremation. The work was over late in the night. No one could speak anything. In fact, none of us had any words. Our group's backbone had broken. We didn't know how to stand now. The whole night we were just in the car on the national highway. I tried to break the silence.

"We have to perform his rituals", I said with a sad voice

"Yes, I am going to ask the priest to come tomorrow and tell us what to do" Raghav said as we didn't have any idea of any death rituals. We had never performed any of those in our past. As we were the only family Mayank had, we had to do it for his soul.

The next day we were having a discussion with the priest about the rituals when someone knocked the door. Rohan went out to find out who it was. He came inside with a man with a black coat. According to his dressing style we could guess that he was a lawyer.

"Hello every one, I am Mayank's lawyer", He introduced himself

"Please have a seat sir", Neel told gently

"I got the information about his sudden death. I have his will ready. If I have your permission then I can read it out." He said very softly

"Yes, sure sir. You can go ahead." Rohan said

The lawyer read out the will and it made my blood run cold. My respect for Mayank touched the skies. He had made Aditi, Sweety and Neel the nominee for his house. The stores were given to Raghav and the rest of the property went into the orphanage fund, we had visited. Neel was sitting in the corner of a room holding Reshma tight. Reshma walked slowly towards us and fell on the ground unconscious.

One loss was unbearable how I could bear the two big losses now. The happenings had drained out my patience. I took a decision to stop working for any political party. I took the decision on behalf of all my friends. I didn't want to lose anyone else. The political party leader came to us requesting us to take part in the party work, but I stood strong to my decision. We were the strongest and the most dangerous party workers he could ever have. After all we had slogged ourselves for months performing all the risky activities. So he had even offered us huge amounts of hard cash. But it stood nowhere after the loss of Mayank. I had decided all of us would leave the path of violence and lead a peaceful life. All had happily agreed with me. Since then we never had parties, no discos and no street fights. I dropped the revolvers into a river which drowned all our criminal activities. I stopped drinking but sometimes I took the help of alcohol when I missed Mayank and Salu a lot. I tried to be a good boy. The spoilt brat was trying to do something good now. I took care of the group and encouraged them to work for their future.

* * * *

Chapter - 31

25th of November - Salu's first birthday after her death

Hey my princess, Happy Birthday. I am missing you a lot today. Do you remember? I had promised you to celebrate your birthday with you in a grand way. I am sorry for not keeping my promise of spending your birthday with you. But I promise you that I will celebrate it in a grand way without tears in my eyes.

I got up early in the morning around 4.00 am. I didn't want to be late for the sunrise. Salu always got upset when I was late so I didn't want to make her upset today. I wore the jeans and the formal shirt she had gifted me while leaving Bhubaneswar. I accelerated my bike towards the hotel where she had stayed. I waited for few minutes in front of the gate, my eyes waiting for her although I knew she would never come. After a few minutes I moved towards the temple on the hill where we had seen the sun rise together.

The sun came up. I folded my hands closing my eyes as she had done it instead of my usual habit of telling good morning to Mr. Sun. It was difficult this time. Last time she was with me but I was all alone this time. I walked slowly towards the pond where we had dropped coins for our wishes. I could see the same priest coming towards me. But he didn't tell me anything this time. I took out two coins from my wallet. One was for me and the other for my Salu. I dropped the first coin for her and the second one for me. I closed my eyes and asked for the wish. I knew what she would have asked. I wished to keep her soul always with me. Then I dropped the coin for me. Last time I was very selfish and I was really ashamed of myself when I read her last letter. This time I wished something different. I wished that my baby should be happy wherever she is.

I walked towards the place where we had spent some time together. I sat down on the rock thinking about the good times we had spent together. I took out my wallet where I always had her photo along with my parents.

I looked at it and started speaking to her. After some time I felt as if she said something.

"I am missing you Prince" she said. I knew it was my illusion but I am sure wherever she was she wanted to talk to me.

My next job was to call up Rohan for her birthday party. Rohan was shocked at my request, but he agreed to help me in the arrangement. This time I ordered for a dark chocolate cake, her favourite but it was of a large sized than I usually ordered. There were all types of alcohol on the table but I didn't touch any. I was not going to make her unhappy at least by consuming alcohol on her birthday. I didn't cry. I knew my Salu gets upset when she finds tears in my eyes. And I was not going to make her low spirited doing that.

After the party I decided to visit the orphanage, her favourite place. I took her birthday cake and purchased some other food stuff for the kids. I also bought new clothes and toys for the kids before getting into the orphanage. As soon as we entered the manager saw us and came to us with a jolly smile. He held my hand and took me in. I handed over the cakes and other stuffs to him.

"There is a bad news sir" I said

"What can be worse than losing such a sweet girl" He said as he meant Salu

"Sir…" I wanted to speak but I fumbled I don't know why

"Sir some people shoot Mayank. He is no more with us" Raghav said pressing my shoulder hard, endeavouring to control his vehemence.

"Why does the Lord do this to good people" he said looking up into the sky.

"Sir, he has donated some of his property to the orphanage fund." I said and asked Reshma to hand over the papers to the manager. She followed my instructions and a deviating silence captured the office room. I made an effort to crack the silence.

"Today is Salu's birthday" I said attempting my best to smile which obviously it looked fake.

"Beta, Kids are missing her a lot" he said

"I am also…" I stopped midway. I didn't want to cry and make my Salu upset. I went out of the office room and started playing with the kids.

The others kept watching me from a distance. I played with the three months old kid, my baby's favorite child in the orphanage. I took him into my arms and started speaking to him about Salu. After a considerable amount of time I moved towards my group. As I reached the group I could feel some one pulling my jeans from behind. I turned to see who it was. It was the same seven years old kid who had asked me about Salu when I had visited the orphanage before to hand over Salu's cheque to the manager. I bent down on my knee.

"Where is Salu di? I am missing her." He said and I didn't know what to speak

"Today is your Salu di's birthday. And she has sent some gifts for you." I said. I indicated Raghav to bring a t-shirt from the bunch of clothes I had brought for the kids and some cake for the kid. The kid ran to the garden and plucked a rose, and then came back to me. I handed over the t-shirt and fed him some cake. He handed over the rose to me.

"Tell her happy birthday. And tell her that I am missing her a lot. Give the rose to Salu di" he said

"She is missing you too my dear" I said. He kissed me on both my cheeks.

"One is for you and another is for Salu di" he spoke innocently and ran away happily with his gift. I got up and moved toward the gate with the group after telling bye to the manager and the kids.

I reached the gate where Neel and Raghav were already waiting for me and other members of the group. They could not see me talking to the child. So, they had left the place. I could see the numbed eyes of Raghav and the tear filled eyes of Neel. I tried to avoid any emotions and keep myself jolly. Although days had passed but Salu's innocent face and her drenched blue eyes had not allowed me to close my eyes.

"Let's go now. It's already late" I said and approached the car but Neel stopped me holding my hand.

"Gyan…" She said and hugged me hard. I could feel her tears wetting my shirt. I could not control my tears anymore. Although I tried to stop them, they rolled over my cheeks.

"I am missing her…" I said and went inside the car.

* * * *

"Hey my Prince" a voice struck my ear drums as I got up from my bed to see who it was

"Salu..." I said as my mouth remained open. She sat next to me. I made an effort to get up from my bed but she didn't allow me to do that.

"Baby, I know you are very angry with me for breaking all my promises made to you" she said and moved her hand over my head as she always did when she was with me.

"No my baby...." I exerted myself to speak but she stopped me again putting her finger on my lips.

"I am so sorry my Prince...please forgive me no" she said in a very innocent voice using the word "NO" as she used to do most of the times.

"I am not angry with you" I said

"I know it baby. You are too good to get angry with me. I want to sleep now Prince" She said and kissed me on my forehead. Then she kept her head resting on my chest. I wanted to talk to her but she stopped me again using her fingers on my lips. I loved it when she slept on my heart. I allowed her to sleep. I hugged her hard and kissed her on her forehead. I wanted to keep her with me forever.

Suddenly my eyes opened with the noise of my alarm clock. I looked into my cell phone. It flashed a reminder-HAPPY ANNIVERSARY SALU AND GYAN. It was 1st of April, 2011. It was our second anniversary and I had to spend it alone. But I decided to spend it in good spirits.

I freshened up and went to the temple as I had done on her birthday. I dropped coins and asked the lord for her Soul's happiness. I ordered for a dark chocolate cake for her. Now Mayank was not there to spend it with me so I had decided to spend it in solitude. I cut the cake and wished her happy anniversary.

Last year I was spending this time with Mayank, Minti and my Salu but this year no one was there to share the happiness of my anniversary. I was missing the fort visit. I was missing her holding my hand. I missed the heart shaped parathas and the toast on which she had written LOVE YOU PRINCE, for the breakfast. I was missing the one day visit to Rajasthan. I was missing her beautiful blue eyes.

At the midnight I accelerated my bike to the place where we had counted stars. The rock was still in its own place. I parked my bike on the road and slept on it and started counting stars. I had counted 517 stars. I wanted to tell I have won but there was no one to listen. I could still feel her heart beat besides me. I came back home with a two minutes noodle from the same 24*7 store. I prepared it with the help of the coffee heater she had given me. I ate half of it and left the rest on the plate for her.

I went to my bed and opened the album flipping through her photos. She looked cute. I picked up my cell phone and went to my contact list. I searched for Salu's number which still existed in my phone book. I selected the options which had an option of sending a text message. I created a message *"Angel, Happy Anniversary...I tried a lot to live my life without you but* ***I still miss you****..."* I sent the message to her number.

* * * *

Epilogue

I looked at my watch. It had struck 4.00 am in the morning. My head was dipped down. After a long time I completely got indulged in my past again. I looked at Lucy's face. I could see her eyes numbed.

"I told you, it's a very pathetic past" I said to make her feel better. She didn't speak anything. She came closer to me. I felt uncomfortable. She held my hand and took me to the entrance of the bogie.

"You are very lovable. I am sure, Salu was really a lucky girl to get a boyfriend in you", she said

"But…." I tried to speak but she placed her finger on my lips as Salu used to do it.

"It's not at all a pathetic one dear. I am so happy and lucky to meet someone so good on this train" she said and came closer to me. It reduced my comfort zone. She took my forehead near her lips and kissed. For the first time after Salu's death I felt something good. I hugged her hard and cried to emit my emotions. I felt relaxed we walked back to our seat.

"Hey Gyan, I need a permission from you", she asked very innocently

"What permission do you need?" I asked

"I really feel like knowing about all other members of your group, please" She said with a childish voice. I could not stop myself from answering to her questions.

"What happened to Reshma after Mayank's death?" she said as her voice seemed very keen knowing about Reshma

"She is continuing her studies and she has taken up a part time job just to avoid Mayank's thoughts", I said

"And what about the other girls", she fired her questions

"Neel's dad had come to meet her and take her back home but she didn't want to leave her friends. Sweety has been regularly visiting her parents. All three have been helping out Raghav in his stores" I said

"What happened with Raghav and Rohan? Are they paired up with anyone?" She asked

"Yes Rohan has paired up with Aditi and Raghav has paired up with Neel. They are very happy together. Rohan has also been helping Raghav in his business." I said

"Is Raghav still frustrated with his business?" she asked

"No, he is walking in the footsteps of Mayank. He has bought five new stores and working very efficiently", I said

"Do you all guys still get together?" she asked and I felt she was not going to stop asking questions

"Yes, in the weekends we meet along with Reshma. We miss Mayank all the time we meet but….." I said and stopped. She didn't force me to continue. She probably knew it was hurting me badly.

"I want to always stay with you Gyan" she said and I could not understand a single word of her statement.

"What?" I asked with a surprise

"Nothing, sleep now I am going to talk to you in the morning" she said and went back to her for sleep.

"But it's already morning", I spoke

"Go to sleep after you get up I am going to talk to you" she said and pulled the blanket over her. I went to my berth and slept.

The next morning when my eyes opened I found Lucy standing besides my berth and looking at me.

"Good Morning Mr. Gyan", she said

"Good Morning", I replied

"Would you like to have some coffee?" She asked as I could find an extra bit of concern in her voice.

"Yes I would love to ma'am" I said with a smile. She took out the cap of her thermo flask to give me some coffee.

I enjoyed the day with her. The rest of her group members were amazed at our chemistry. I could see them teasing Lucy and surprisingly, she reacted positively. We exchanged our phone numbers. She had to get down two hour before me. At the arrival of her station she held my hand and hugged me.

"Hey Gyan, I will try coming to you" She said and I could never understand her statements sometimes.

I reached Delhi at 4.00 pm and took an auto rickshaw to my uncle's place in Malaviya Nagar. It took me two hours to reach my uncle's place. All the time Lucy's thought had been revolving round my brain. It was the first time that some other girl was brought into my thought process other than Salu. My aunt was very happy welcoming me. I touched her feet and entered the house. My phone beeped with the arrival of a text message. I took out the cell phone to see who it was. The screen flashed Lucy. I opened the message. "Gyan, I had a chat with Dad. He agreed for my transfer to your University in Odisha. I will be there with you by next month." I just smiled and kept the cell phone in my pocket.

* * * *